HANUKKAH PARODIES

Hanukkah Parodies:

Short Plays for the Festival of Lights

Shoshana Hantman

Sidney Books

NEW YORK

www.sidneybooks.com

To contact the author, write to RabbiHantman@sidneybooks.com

Cover design: Julie Leiman Weaver
(www.coroflot.com/julieleimanweaverillustration)
Interior typeface: Book Antiqua
Cover typefaces: OptimusPrinceps Semibold, Black Jack, and Bernhard Modern Standard

ISBN: 978-0-9913512-1-3

First Sidney Books trade paperback edition November 2018

10 9 8 7 6 5 4 3 2 1

This book is dedicated to my cousins,
Ioannis Mansalis and Roberta Goodman Mansalis,

and to my good friends,
Maria Lambros Kannen and Michael Kannen

-- magnificent examples of the collaboration
of Greek and Jewish culture

Acknowledgments

My husband of twenty-eight years, Richard Weill, has given me the gift of time, and in addition he's a valuable creative and technical resource. He has a keen ear for dialogue and a great sense of pacing. Rich is generous with his attention and support, and, like my previous books, this one wouldn't exist without him.

Many friends have shared their knowledge and advice: Amy Hersh, Sue Frank, Seth Walter, Shari Schwartz Walter, Rick Libowitz, Joel Hoffman, Helen Miller, Jane Lamphier Atkin, Kristin Judd Horowitz, Arthur Gould, Elissa Wald, Diane Snyder Brown, Bonnie Jean Clancy, Joe Ebbinger, Stefania Rishel, Javier Cabrera and Karen Sussan.

For many years, my Hebrew school students have been reading my scripts in class, and offering helpful suggestions and feedback. They are too many to list here, but they know who they are.

Julie Leiman Weaver created a very beautiful cover, and I thank her.

My children, Mollie and Isaac Hantman-Weill, are patient and kind with a mother who sometimes tells them to go away and be quiet. They are writers themselves, and they understand.

October 2018

CONTENTS

Introduction

The Jewish Festival of Lights is a widely misunderstood and well-loved holiday. Occurring at roughly the same time as Christmas, it scrambles to compete, and thereby draws constant comparisons which obscure its real character.

The events that Hanukkah commemorates happened just a bit too late for inclusion in the TaNa"Kh, the Hebrew Bible. Alexander III of Macedon had conquered much of Asia and northeast Africa by 326 BCE, suffusing Greek culture into many societies that were incorporated into his empire. Generally, this blending, or syncretism, was a powerful fertilizer for the progress of the arts, sciences and philosophy.

After Alexander's death in 323 BCE, his kingdom fractured into several vast blocs, including the Babylon-based Seleucid Empire. This grew to include Anatolia, Mesopotamia, Persia, and Judea, among other areas. In 175 BCE, the Seleucid heir Antiochus IV seized power. Some of these ethnically distinct areas became Hellenized – heavily influenced by Greek culture. Some didn't. In any case, it's incorrect to refer to this empire as "the Greeks" and this book does not.

Probably emotionally unstable to start with, Antiochus tried to exalt himself by invading Ptolemaic Egypt. His ambitions began to crumble when ascendant Rome pushed back, and Antiochus' military efforts became more and more expensive.

The mad emperor spied an attractive source of funds in his vassal city of Jerusalem. Jewish politics were dominated by the priestly class, the kohaneem, who were wealthy, and who relished the sophisticated Greek culture more than the average Jew. There was jockeying for position among the kohaneem, and some of them were willing to pay Antiochus to replace the incumbent High Priest with *their* guy, Jason. The emperor cooperated, and, a short time later, another aspiring High Priest named Menelaus offered

Antiochus a better price ... and he replaced Jason. It was classic pay-to-play.

Imprudently, Menelaus pawned Temple treasures in order to pay the emperor. Many among the Jewish community were enraged, and supported Jason's efforts to get his old office back. Briefly, they were successful, until the emperor reinstated Menelaus. Menelaus, backed by Antiochus, took revenge on the populace by forcing on them more Hellenic practices than they wanted – like placing a statue of Zeus in the Holy Temple itself.

This offensive move, along with new imperial edicts outlawing such essential Jewish practices like Torah study, Shabbat observance and circumcision, was the flashpoint that prompted the small-town kohayn, Matityahu (why call him by the Greek version, Mattathias?) to assemble a band of Jewish guerilla fighters in 167 BCE to oppose the Seleucid Empire. The second book of Maccabees, an Alexandrian work composed decades later, tells us that among those responding to Matityahu's call "Let all who are for the Lord follow me!" were his five sons, Shimon, Yohanan, Yonatan, Eliezer and Yehudah (Judah). That same legend says that the last thing Matiyahu did before forming the rebel army, was to kill an imperial soldier who was forcing the Jews of Modi'in to offer sacrifices to a Greek idol.

The newly-formed rebel army became known at some point as the 'Maccabees.' This name may derive from the Hebrew *makevet* meaning hammer, or be an acronym for 'Matityahu Kohayn ben Yohanan." A popular theory is that it's the acrostic of a phrase from Exodus, chapter 15, verse 11, *Mee kamoha ba-elim, Adonai?* (Who is like You among the gods, Adonai?). In any event, that wasn't the family's name. Their name was Hasmon or Hashmon, which may reflect their ancestry in the tribe of Shimon. The dynasty of leaders this family produced after winning the Maccabean revolt is known as the Hasmonean Dynasty.

This remarkable military family engaged many enemy generals – Nicanor, Gorgias, Apollonius, among others – continuing their anti-pagan campaign over a large geographical area. Their biggest victory, the re-conquest of Jerusalem, culminated in 164 BCE. Judah's forces took control of the Temple, purged it of the Zeus cult, purified and re-dedicated it to Jewish service. This dedication – which is called in Hebrew *Hanukkah* – took place on the 25th of the month of Kislev.

After making a historic treaty with the Roman Republic in 161 BCE, Judah resumed the fight against the Seleucids. He was killed in the battle of Elasa in 160. Eliezer had died in action previously. The brothers Jonathan, Yohanan, and Simon carried on, winning independence for the Jewish nation several years later.

After the external enemy was defeated, the Maccabee leadership engaged with the Jewish priests who persisted in their Hellenistic loyalties. The struggle in the Seleucid Empire continued, also; the Hanukkah war was complex, not linear.

Neither was the Hasmonean dynasty's legacy. Once in control, they continued their drive for religious purity, oppressing dissidents and even forcing the conversion of the Idumeans to Judaism – the only such instance in Jewish history. This particular outrage ultimately had a disastrous result. One of those forced converts produced a son who would become the worst despot to reign in Jerusalem: King Herod.

The war was one of many Jewish rebellions against the empires that occupied Judea – and the only successful one. Independence under the Hasmonean dynasty lasted a hundred years, ending under the heel of the Romans. It was in Roman times, by the way, that the legend of the cruse of oil that lasted eight days began. A festival celebrating a successful rebellion would not have been good for the Jews at that time. So an anodyne miracle became the focus of Hanukkah. The festival of lights at the dark time of year has endured since then.

Popular memory does to Hanukkah what it has always done. It enshrines what captures our imagination, and drops the rest. If the Hasmoneans were here today, they would be intolerant fundamentalists campaigning against what we know is true religious freedom. So, we take from their story what we need now: inspiration to guard and celebrate our identity. It's a valuable, irreplaceable role. It's how cultural history must function.

Monty Python and the Holy Oil

– a legend of the Knights of the Renowned Temple –

The Monty Python comedy troupe that sprang into life on the United Kingdom's BBC-TV in 1969 resonated mightily in the hearts and souls of humor lovers everywhere. Vulgar, surreal, and irreverent, to say the least, the Pythons smashed through conventions and satisfied a desperate need for rebellion against oppressive, irrelevant authority.

Jewish comedy has played the same role for a long time. Even before the comic outrages of the Marx Brothers, Mel Brooks, and Lenny Bruce, Purim shpiels have been snapping at power figures and institutions since medieval times at least. I read somewhere that in sixteenth-century Germany, Purim celebrations got so out of hand that government authorities had to close them down at times.

My personal reference point is Purim; always has been. Most holidays need a touch of it. So this volume opens with a gallop down the misty paths of legendary England, in the company of a hapless General Judah of the castle Kvetchalot.

SOLDIER
JUDAH
SHEEPISH
JUSTICE GINSBURG (RBG)
HEAD KNIGHT
ASSYRIAN
ELIEZER
KLUTZ
SHIMON

(Trumpet fanfare. Clop clop clop)

SOLDIER	Halt! Who goes there?
JUDAH	It is I, Judah, son of Matityahu Pendragon, from the castle of Kvetchalot, general of the Jewish Army, defeater of the Assyrians!
SOLDIER	And who's that?
JUDAH	This is my trusty squire, Sheepish. We have ridden the length and breadth of the Judean Hills in search of commanders who will join my court.
SOLDIER	What? Ridden on a horse?
JUDAH	Yes.
SOLDIER	Why, you're using coconuts. You've got two empty coconut halves and you're bangin' 'em together!
JUDAH	We have ridden from the Jerusalem's Holy Temple, where we defeated the army of King Antiochus and re-dedicated the Temple, through –
SOLDIER	Where'd you get them coconuts?
SHEEPISH	We found them.
SOLDIER	Found them? There's no coconuts in the land of

Israel.

JUDAH   What do you mean?

SOLDIER   Nobody grows coconuts here.

JUDAH   They may have been carried here. By a native spe-
                cies of bird. Such as the ... chicken.

SOLDIER   You're suggesting that a chicken carried a coconut
                to the Judean Hills?

SHEEPISH   It doesn't really matter.

SOLDIER   How could a chicken carry something heavier than
                itself, even assuming it could grip a coconut --

JUDAH   Be quiet! I order you to be quiet!

SOLDIER   You order me, eh? Who do you think you are?

JUDAH   I am the General of the Judean Army!

SOLDIER   Well, how did you become General, then? I didn't
                vote for you.

JUDAH   The Lady of the Bench ...

(Angels sing)

                ... clad in the purest shimmering black robe, and a
                very nice lacy collar as well, held aloft Excalibur
                from the bosom of the Court, signifying that by di-
                vine providence, I, Judah, was to carry Excalibur.

(singing stops)

SOLDIER   You can't expect to command the Jewish Army just
                because some old judge threw a sword at you.

JUDAH   Shut up, will you? Just shut up!

SOLDIER   Supreme power derives from a mandate from the
                masses, not some farcical legalistic ceremony ...

Oh great heavens, what's that?

(Angels begin singing again)

RBG	Judah the Maccabee!
JUDAH	The Lady of the Bench! Your Worship, you honor me with your ...
RBG	Oh, stop groveling. I can't stand groveling. And stop that singing, I can't hear myself think!

(Singing stops)

JUDAH	Sorry.
RBG	And don't apologize. Now pay attention. I have come here to instruct you on your sacred quest.
JUDAH	What is my sacred quest, your honorable worship?
RBG	Take with you the Knights of the Renowned Temple, and seek ye a cruse of holy oil with which to light the Eternal Light.
JUDAH	But, Your Honor, what is this holy oil? Where shall I find it? And for that matter, where will I find the Knights of the Renowned Temple?
RBG	It's a little bottle with an O-U on it. Try a supermarket.
JUDAH	But where are the Knights that I seek?
RBG	You hopeless twit. Your brothers! The men who fought with you against the Assyrians!
JUDAH	You mean Sir Jonathan the Brave, Sir Shimon the Wise, Sir Eliezer the Pure, and Sir Yohanan the Not Quite So Pure As Eliezer?
RBG	Yes, of course.
JUDAH	I haven't seen them since we re-dedicated the

Temple.

RBG   The Knights have been captured by *(pause)* Klutz the Enchanter.

SHEEPISH   But where can this Enchanter be found, Your Honor?

RBG   Beyond the Sea of Ridiculous Amounts of Salt, you will find the Enchanter, guarded by the Knights Who Say Nu. All right, you have your instructions. Begone, for there is no time to lose.

JUDAH   Sheepish, we must seek the Enchanter and rescue the Knights of the Renowned Temple. Away!

(Trumpet fanfare. Clop clop clop)

SHEEPISH   Sire, hark! Yonder stand a troupe of knights all clad in grey, with rams' horns upon their heads!

HEAD KNIGHT Nu!

JUDAH   Who be-est thou, Sir Knight?

HEAD KNIGHT We are the knights who say Nu.

JUDAH   And why do you say that?

HEAD KNIGHT Nu?

JUDAH   Well, never mind then. I am General Judah, son of Matityahu Pendragon, and I come to seek the freedom of my brothers, Sir Jonathan the Brave, Sir Shimon the Wise, Sir Eliezer the Pure, and Sir Yohanan the Not Quite So Pure As Eliezer.

HEAD KNIGHT Nu?

JUDAH   Please don't say that again. We are but travelers …

HEAD KNIGHT We will say Nu until you appease us.

JUDAH   Well, what do you want?

HEAD KNIGHT We want …

(Dramatic chord)

HEAD KNIGHT A tchotchke!

JUDAH   A what?

HEAD KNIGHT Nu? Nu? Nu?

JUDAH   Ow! No! Please! No more! We will bring you a … tchotchke.

HEAD KNIGHT You must bring us a tchotchke, or you shall never pass through this wood … alive.

JUDAH   O Knights of Nu, you are just and fair. We will return with a tchotchke.

HEAD KNIGHT One that looks nice.

JUDAH   Of course.

HEAD KNIGHT And not schmaltzy.

JUDAH   Yes.

HEAD KNIGHT Nu? So go already.

JUDAH   *(quietly)* Sheepish, might you happen to have any sort of tchotchke on you?

SHEEPISH   Well, Sire, not much. Oh! Perhaps this will do. It's a small ceramic dreidel with Disney characters painted on it.

JUDAH   Sheepish, you have saved the day! The Knights will treasure it. Hand it over.

SHEEPISH   But my Bubbie gave it to me.

JUDAH   Bubbie will understand. Let's have it. Oh, good Sir Knight!

HEAD KNIGHT Nu?

JUDAH   With reverence and respect, we bring you this tchotchke.

HEAD KNIGHT   Not bad. General Judah! You have triumphed. Having acquired a tchotchke, and presented it to the Knights Who Say Nu, you have proved yourself worthy of the hand of Princess Judith of Bethulia.

JUDAH   The … what? The hand of a Princess? I'm not on a quest for a Princess. I'm trying to rescue my brother knights, and obtain a small bottle of holy oil.

HEAD KNIGHT   You're not on a quest to win the Princess?

JUDAH   No, you must be thinking of someone else.

HEAD KNIGHT   Just wait a minute. Let me check my notes. Didn't you say you were General Nicanor, the son of Patroclus, sent by the Assyrian king to defeat the Jewish Army at the Battle of Adasa?

JUDAH   Sir Knight, I am sure I said I was Judah, son of Matityahu, commander of the Jewish Army.

HEAD KNIGHT   Ah, that explains it. Judah, Judith.

JUDAH   Very similar, Sir Knight. But tell me, if you will, what is to become of the Princess Judith of Bethulia?

HEAD KNIGHT   Her destiny is to welcome General Nicanor with strong   drink, wait till he passes out, and then cut off his head.

JUDAH   Blimey. Glad we dodged *that*, eh, Sheepish?

SHEEPISH   It would have been unpleasant, sire.

HEAD KNIGHT   Off you go, then. You'll find the Castle Oy through that wood, where sits Klutz the Enchanter. Ta.

(Clop clop clop)

SHEEPISH	It's the Castle Oy, my liege, but a moment's ride hence!
JUDAH	And well-fortified, Sheepish, with armed and contemptuous Assyrian soldiers.
SHEEPISH	There! Look!
JUDAH	It's an inscription. What language is that?
SHEEPISH	It's Yiddish, my liege. It says: "He who is valiant and pure of spirit may find the holy oil within the Castle of Oy."
ASSYRIAN	Oi!
JUDAH	Soldier! How dare you profane this place with your presence, when your forces have been defeated time and again by the might of the Maccabees!
ASSYRIAN	*(in a French accent)* I *greps* at your militia, cheesy duck-faced Hebrew!
JUDAH	In the name of the Lord, we demand entrance to this castle!
ASSYRIAN	Get lost, silly bed-wetting meshuggeners! Depart before we launch deadly Ashkenazic missiles in your general direction!
JUDAH	Oh, a culture war, is it? Well, then! With our shields of David and our swords of steel, we shall take this castle by force! To arms, Sheepish!

(Thud)

SHEEPISH	Sire, take cover! They're launching great lumps of gefilte fish!
JUDAH	Run away, run away!

ASSYRIAN	Yes, run away, dappy Judean nitwits, before we make kreplach out of your gall bladders! Aaahh …
SHEEPISH	What's happening to the Assyrians, sire? And what's that terrible smell?
JUDAH	It smells like … I believe that's the odor of grated horse-radish!
SHEEPISH	The soldiers have collapsed over the battlements!
JUDAH	Without a doubt, Sir Yohanan the Not Quite So Pure as Eliezer has overcome the Assyrians from inside the Castle Oy. Bravely done, my brother knight! Sheepish, prepare to storm the gatehouse and rescue the Judean commanders!

(trumpet fanfare)

ELIEZER	General Judah has come to free us from the wicked Klutz the Enchanter!
KLUTZ	Not so fast, Judean.
SHEEPISH	Look, it's Klutz the Enchanter, keeper of the Drawbridge of Death.
JUDAH	What's he doing here?
SHEEPISH	He asks each traveler four questions …
ELIEZER	Four questions?
KLUTZ	Hush! He who would cross the Drawbridge of Death must answer me these questions four, ere the castle he score.
SHEEPISH	What if you get a question wrong?
KLUTZ	Then you are cast into the Gorge of Eternal Perelman.
JUDAH	Right, then. Let's have it. I am not afraid!

KLUTZ   What ... is your name?

JUDAH   My name is Judah Maccabee, son of Matityahu Pendragon.

KLUTZ   What ... is your quest?

JUDAH   To free my brother knights and search out a jar of the Holy Oil.

KLUTZ   What ... is the purpose of the Holy Oil?

JUDAH   To light the eternal light in the Renowned Temple. What's the last question?

KLUTZ   Mah nishtana ha-layla ha-zeh?

ELIEZER   Oh, time out, time out! That's a Passover question, totally inappropriate for a Hanukkah parody.

JUDAH   You have forfeited the drawbridge, enchanter! Move aside, for we now storm the castle to free Sir Sir Jonathan the Brave, Sir Shimon the Wise, Sir Eliezer the Pure, and Sir Yohanan the Not Quite So Pure As Eliezer, and to gain the Holy Oil.

SHIMON   Brother Judah! We have long languished in the castle keep, awaiting rescue. And now you are here! Tell us how you have come to Castle Oy.

JUDAH   The gracious Lady of the Bench appeared to me ...

(Angels sing)

               ... and, clad in the purest shimmering black robe, and a very nice lacy collar as well, gave me the sword Excalibur, and told me to seek my brother knights and find a cruse of Holy Oil.

SHIMON   The Holy Oil?

JUDAH   Yes.

SHIMON   Well, what Holy Oil is that?

JUDAH   Holy Oil, that's it.

SHIMON   But did she want corn oil? Cottonseed oil? Saf-
             flower oil? Did she mean oil intended as biofuel,
             food supplements, or emollients? Maybe she wants
             pumpkin-seed oil, macadamia oil, or flaxseed oil,
             which is high in omega-3. Alternatively, she may
             have been requesting canola oil, neem oil, or even
             whale oil. Did the lady clarify whether she wanted
             organic oil at all? Perhaps she only wanted to lu-
             bricate an automobile engine with motor oil. Or
             she has a squeaky door-hinge, and needs some
             WD-40.

JUDAH   Enough, Sir Shimon! The Lady of the Bench explic-
             itly stated that the oil was for the eternal light in the
             Renowned Temple.

SHIMON   Oh. Well, you didn't say that.

JUDAH   I thought I did.

SHIMON   Right, then. She wants olive oil for that.

ELIEZER   Olive oil? Like this here?

SHEEPISH   My liege! Sir Eliezer holds the sacred cruse of Holy
             Oil!

JUDAH   Brilliant!

SHIMON   Where'd you get that?

ELIEZER   In the eastern Judean Desert, by the Sea of a Ridicu-
             lous Amount of Salt, lies the Wadi Qumran. There,
             in caves full of sacred manuscripts stored in
             earthen vessels, I was led by the mystical Melvin of
             the Brooks to a spot where this single cruse of oil
             was hidden – waiting, as it were, for a pure-hearted
             knight of the Renowned Temple to discover it and
             carry it to the re-dedicated Temple in Jerusalem.

(Angels sing)

SHEEPISH   It's the Lady of the Bench! She's back again.

JUDAH   Your Honor!

RBG   Eliezer, you don't need me to remind you that it's a sin to tell a lie.

ELIEZER   Sweet Lady of the Bench, I didn't know you were listening.

RBG   That shouldn't make any difference. Now, Eliezer, where did you find the Holy Oil?

ELIEZER   At the supermarket. In the kosher aisle.

RBG   That's better.

JUDAH   Knights of valor! Our sacred quest is achieved. We shall bring this sacred oil to the Renowned Temple, and light the Eternal Light of the Lord.

SHIMON   And thence to return to our Castle of Kvetchalot, ever prepared to answer the call of the Lord in service to the Jewish people.

SHEEPISH   For never were there so loyal or so brave as the brave Knights of the Renowned Table. The Judeans stand ready to follow you, General Judah, unto the furthest reaches of the realm, for the glory of the Torah!

RBG   What you actually need to do, is to go back to Jerusalem, light the eternal light, and then get to work repairing the other destruction the Assyrians inflicted on the Holy Land.

ELIEZER   What do you mean, Lady of the Bench?

RBG   You have to rebuild the mills and the mines, quarry the stone, repair the roads, muck the barns, plow the fields, harvest the grain, haul the water, grind the corn, and winnow the wheat.

(Pause)

ELIEZER   Is there someone else up there we could talk to?

RBG   No.

SHIMON   On second thought, let's not go to Jerusalem. It's a silly place.

JUDAH   The Lady of the Bench makes a valid point. The trouble with the Seleucid Empire began with local unrest which prompted administrative punishment upon the Judeans. The chaos which followed disrupted economic function, resulting in crumbling infrastructure. Much hard work lies ahead if we are to restore a fully-functioning society.

SHEEPISH   How do you know so much about macroeconomics?

JUDAH   Well, you have to know these things when you're a general, you know.

Antiochus Roadshow

— a Public Television Hanukkah —

I like to be honest, when it's convenient. So I'll be honest here. I was watching public television one day, avoiding some task or other, when this title popped into my head. I knew immediately that I had to write a Hanukkah-themed parody of *Antiques Road-show,* the program that visits various communities, inviting people to bring in their attic treasures for professional valuation and story-telling.

Israel is well-known as a paradise for antiquities enthusiasts. So herein, Israelis from the town of Modi'in present items they've picked up here and there. Appraisers have a look and offer their opinions. Although the appraisers you'll see here are well-educated about Jewish history, you are cautioned not to take these artifacts too seriously.

MARK WALBERG
APPRAISER 1
RONIT
HANAN
APPRAISER 2
APPRAISER 3
AYALA
APPRAISER 4
DANNY
APPRAISER 5
SARAH

MARK   Welcome to Antiochus Roadshow! Today, we're
              excited to pass through Modi'in, about halfway be-
              tween Tel Aviv and Jerusalem on Highway 445 in
              central Israel.   This modern city of 92,000 dates
              back only to 1985, when Maccabi, the international
              Jewish sports organization, started its construction.
              But the ancient town goes way back to before the
              Common Era.   In fact, Modi'in was the hometown
              of none other than Matitiyahu, the revolutionary
              leader and father of the Maccabee brothers!   The
              Roadshow is here in Modi'in to discover Israel's
              hidden treasures.

              We have a sold-out crowd here in Modi'in's cul-
              tural auditorium, and they're pretty excited to see
              us.

WHOLE CAST   *(shouting)* Welcome to Modi'in!

MARK   One big find here is a small clay statuette brought
              in by Ronit.

APPRAISER 1   So, tell us about this statuette, Ronit.

RONIT   Well, originally, my great-grandfather found it
              while he was digging a foundation for his garden
              shed. This was about 1946. He was using an ordi-

nary hand-shovel and a pick, and the family story is that, when he came across this little figure in the limestone, he just threw it aside.

APPRAISER 1   It doesn't show any sign of breakage.

RONIT   No, it seems to be in good shape.

APPRAISER 1   This has been in your family ever since then?

RONIT   Yes, my grandmother kept it in her china cabinet, and when I got married, she gave it to me. She said it was for good luck.

APPRAISER 1   This little fellow is made of terracotta. We'll never know the identity of the artist, but he, or she, almost certainly lived in the Parthian kingdom during the Hellenistic period, the three centuries before the Common Era. The statue is about ten inches high, and it's a man in simple clothing, sporting a full beard. His arms are held high above his head in an attitude of surprise or, perhaps, worship.

RONIT   The Parthian kingdom?

APPRAISER 1   The Parthians were a huge Iranian empire of that time, and the western reaches of that kingdom cover what is now Syria. The big question is how it came to be in Central Israel, and I think we find the answer in this inscription on his back. Do you see these letters here?

RONIT   Oh, yes. Those are letters?

APPRAISER 1   The alphabet is a type of Aramaic script, and the word clearly reads "Epiphanes." This little man is praising the Seleucid emperor Antiochus the Fourth. He was the king who oppressed the Jews so cruelly that he prompted the Maccabean War.

RONIT   *This* little statue? That's been on my dresser all this time?

APPRAISER 1   All this time, he's been worshiping the antagonist of the Hanukkah story.

RONIT   I can hardly believe it!

APPRAISER 1   There's no way to tell twenty-one centuries later, but he could have been on his way to the Temple in Jerusalem. That's where Antiochus had placed a statue of Zeus, and no doubt, plenty of smaller images to adore him. This little man's in excellent condition. Now, what would you guess it's worth?

RONIT   I have no idea. Maybe five hundred shekels?

APPRAISER 1   I estimate that, if you put this up for auction – of course after showing it to the Israel Antiquities Authority which is in charge of all ancient finds – it would sell for, conservatively, twenty to twenty-five thousand shekels.

RONIT   You have got to be kidding!

APPRAISER 1   This is a national treasure, a real piece of history. I would urge you to contact the Israel Museum. You could get an incredible tax break for the donation of this little Parthian.

RONIT   Thank you so much!

(Twinkling sound)

MARK   Parthian terracotta figure. Twenty to twenty-five thousand shekels.

HANAN   My wife and I are in the scrap-metal business, and one day a customer came in with a huge carton of stuff he wanted to unload. It was mostly broken pieces of machinery and tools, but this one seemed a little different.

APPRAISER 2   It's a four-sided metal box with no top and no bottom. The sides have rows of holes with razor-sharp edges. And here we have a handle on top. Did your customer say what it was?

HANAN   Only that his mother brought it here when she left Russia about 1920.

APPRAISER 2   It's very old and partially oxidized.

HANAN   We thought maybe those are air-holes. Maybe it's the frame of a box for transporting small animals. Or maybe a drain of some kind, like you'd put over a pipe at the bottom of a fountain.

APPRAISER 2   The important clue about this item is actually what you told me about its origin. You said your customer's mother bought it over from Russia. So it was important enough to her that she didn't want to leave it behind; something, perhaps, that she used a lot. Not a fountain drain.

HANAN   Maybe it's a tool of some kind.

APPRAISER 2   It *is* a tool. It's a kitchen tool, something the Russian émigré might have used very frequently – but especially on Hanukkah.

HANAN   You mean – you think this is for making latkes?!

APPRAISER 2   That's right! In those days they didn't have food processors. In order to get those potatoes shredded to make latkes, people had to grate them by hand. You'd put this in a bowl, hold the handle with one hand, and scrape the potato against these holes. The shreds would pile up inside the grater.

HANAN   Oh! Well, that's very interesting. I guess a lot of work went into making latkes back then. What do you think this would be worth?

APPRAISER 2   It's not in very good condition, I'm afraid. But if it were, I'd say eight to ten shekels, at a street market.

HANAN   Too bad! Back to the scrap-yard.

(Twinkling sound)

MARK   Russian potato grater. Eight to ten shekels.

APPRAISER 3 This looks very impressive! It's a Hellenistic-era makhaira! How did you come by it?

AYALA   I picked this sword up at a tag-sale in Beit Horon, which is near here, maybe five years ago. The owner said he'd gotten it from an antiquities dealer before the Six-Day War. The trail sort of ends there.

APPRAISER 3 It's either a small sword or a large knife, depending on how you want to look at it. A weapon like this would have been used by a Greek or Persian cavalryman. It's designed to cut rather than thrust; you see it's single-bladed.

AYALA   It's very heavy.

APPRAISER 3 Yes, it has a lot of heft. This was made from a bar or billet of iron and steel, softened in a forge and then hammered into this shape. If you look along here you can see the marks of the hammer.

AYALA   Not very sharp anymore.

APPRAISER 3 No, although we can imagine its original polish, the metal has corroded a lot over the centuries. But the really interesting thing about this weapon is that it comes from Beit Horon. In 166 BCE, Judah Maccabee's forces battled against the Seleucid Army in that very spot.

AYALA   Who won?

APPRAISER 3 The Maccabees. They knew their terrain very well, and were able to outmaneuver the Seleucids, and kill their commander, Seron. It was a decisive victory in the war for Jewish freedom. The rebels never looked back. In 165, they entered Jerusalem, re-dedicating the Temple in the Jewish tradition.

AYALA So it's possible this sword was used in the Battle of Horon?

APPRAISER 3 We can't know for sure. But the age of this makhaira indicates the Hellenistic time period, and the style seems consistent with Seleucid weaponry. I think there's a better than fifty-per-cent chance that the owner of this sword – if he survived – was chased into the Judean hills by the Maccabees.

AYALA That's amazing!

APPRAISER 3 Do you mind my asking how much you paid for it?

AYALA I really splurged. I paid seventy-five shekels for it.

APPRAISER 3 So, knowing what you do now, how much would you guess this makhaira is worth?

AYALA Oh – I couldn't possibly put a price on it.

APPRAISER 3 I agree, that would be hard! But, for insurance purposes, this Hellenist-era sword should be valued in the range of one hundred to one hundred twenty thousand shekels.

AYALA That much! I'm – I'm just – I can't believe it! I've got chills!

APPRAISER 3 Do you think you'll keep it, or sell it?

AYALA I need to think about it. But my heart says to hold on to it.

APPRAISER 3 Thank you for bringing it in today.

(Twinkling sound)

MARK Hellenist-era makhaira. One hundred to one hundred twenty thousand shekels.

DANNY   I found this dreidel a year ago while I was cleaning out my grandparents' apartment in Teaneck, New Jersey. It's still in the original box, but the cover is so worn down I can only see part of a word I believe is "Scharfstein."

APPRAISER 4   This is a dreidel, the toy most closely associated with the celebration of Hanukkah. But, unlike the colorful plastic ones you see these days, this dreidel is made of lead. There's no date on the box, but I would estimate this was made about the year 1935. It's definitely pre-war.

DANNY   Who is 'Scharfstein'?

APPRAISER 4   Fannie and Asher Scharfstein were Russian Jews who immigrated to America in 1922. They were entrepreneurs and, after they arrived in New York, they decided they wanted to manufacture items for Jewish customers, and hit upon the idea of making and selling lead dreidels. Asher found a tool-and-die maker who owned a dreidel casting machine – really! – and Fannie melted lead and poured it into the dreidel-shaped mold. Pretty soon she was turning out seventy-five dreidels an hour.

DANNY   I've seen wooden dreidels, and bronze and silver ones in artist galleries, but never a lead one, other than this.

APPRAISER 4   This would have been the only kind of dreidel you'd see in a Jewish home in the early twentieth century. Eventually, plastic replaced lead, which of course is poisonous to a young child who puts it in his mouth.

DANNY   I guess my grandparents bought this for my mom and her sisters.

APPRAISER 4   They were careful to keep it in the original box, which increases its value.

DANNY   I wonder how well the Scharfsteins did in the dreidel business.

APPRAISER 4   They made enough money to put their boys through college. After serving in World War II, Sol and Bernie went into the family business, which had evolved into Ktav Publishing House. They built it into the country's biggest producer of Hebrew schoolbooks and materials. I'd say the majority of American synagogue students have had Ktav books in their hands, at some time or another.

DANNY   What do you think the dreidel is worth now?

APPRAISER 4   The Scharfsteins sold these for two cents each. Today, with its original box, and in its mint condition, you'll get about fifty dollars for it on eBay.

DANNY   Well, thank you very much.

(Twinkling sound)

MARK   American pre-war lead dreidel, fifty dollars.

APPRAISER 5   You've brought in an item which very rarely seen, if ever. Tell us how you came by it.

SARAH   I was conducting a tour for some foreign visitors outside the walls of the Old City, in Jerusalem. We were a few hundred yards from the New Gate, and the tourists couldn't hear me because of the construction equipment. They're building an addition onto a hospital there. So I said to the tourists, "Let's get a little further from this," and when I turned to lead them away, my foot hit some of the rubble. When I bent down to see if my ankle was bleeding, I saw this. It was covered with dust.

APPRAISER 5   This is a clay jar, about fourteen inches in height. It's nearly round, with a fairly narrow neck and a wide lip. Was it kicked up by the digging equipment, do you think?

SARAH   It must have been.

APPRAISER 5   It has a few hairline cracks, and it's discolored with age, but it's intact. The style strongly suggests that this is an oil jar, and that it dates to the second or third century BCE.

SARAH   It's that old?!

APPRAISER 5   That was my original suspicion. And my suspicion was confirmed when I saw this very faint inscription on the bottom. Are you able to see it?

SARAH   I see some scratches. They look like a couple of rough boxes and lines.

APPRAISER 5   This is actually Hebrew. The ancient Israelites used an Aramaic alphabet, and by the third century were writing letters in a square form, just as the Persians were doing at that time. These letters are mem, qof, daled, shin.

SARAH   "Mikdash"?

APPRAISER 5   And of course, you know what *that* is.

SARAH   The mikdash is the holy place, the sanctuary. The Temple.

APPRAISER 5   Exactly! This jar held oil that was used, or was intended to be used, in the Temple in Jerusalem.

SARAH   Wait a minute! Could this be the oil jar the Maccabees found to light the menorah, when they re-dedicated the Temple! The oil that lasted eight days?

APPRAISER 5   It's a nice thought. But that story about the miracle of the oil was devised several hundred years after the Temple's re-dedication. It was a sort of a cover story. The rabbis knew it would be a bad idea to celebrate the Maccabees' victory over Antiochus' empire. After all, they were living under Roman occupation, and the Romans didn't appreciate rebels. So, the oil legend became the ostensible, the official, reason for celebrating Hanukkah.

SARAH   But then, why is Hanukkah eight days long?

APPRAISER 5   The Maccabees resented that Antiochus had outlawed their favorite holiday, Sukkot, which is eight days long. So they instituted the new festival to be a reflection of Sukkot. Then they had *two* festivals.

SARAH   That's amazing. But what about this jar?

APPRAISER 5   Please put it down, Sarah. This is an extremely precious relic of the Second Temple, which is why we've brought in a security detail to escort it, and you, to the offices of the Antiquities Authority. We are so grateful that you've brought in this ancient oil jar. Without your quick action, it could have been destroyed by those bulldozers. The Israel Museum will find a way to express the State's appreciation to you.

SARAH   Oh! Okay, I guess …

APPRAISER 5   Now, that's something we don't see every day.

(Twinkling sound)

MARK   Second Temple period oil jar. Beyond valuation.

If *you* happen to have some old family heirlooms in the attic, you might want to check if Antiochus Roadshow is coming to your town. I'm Mark Walberg – thanks for watching! See you next time on Antiochus Roadshow.

Make Latkes, Not War

— a sixties Hanukkah –

"Where Have The Hippies Gone?" asks a plaintive bumper sticker I recently saw. I understood it immediately. The hippie generation of the 1960s changed America. Their guiding philosophy of love, acceptance and self-exploration combined with a challenge to the war-supporting, conformist establishment. Nothing would ever be the same. Ethnic diversity became something that should be celebrated, not suppressed into a parve and monolithic society. Questioning authority was no longer an abomination. It became a sanctum.

Of course the hippies were excessive, and their earnestness in retrospect might be laughable. But progress rarely occurs in careful, refined stages. They made our society a better place for individualists, for challengers.

Would Jews with hippie sensibilities have fit into the Maccabee rebellion? The Maccabees were single-minded, fanatical revolutionaries. They may have appreciated passionate support, but they were far from freethinkers. That would have been an odd alliance indeed. But that's why this is just a fantasy.

Where have all the hippies gone? In this skeptical, pessimistic era, I really want them back.

SHALOM
MAYIM
MATITYAHU
JUDAH
MENELAUS
JONATHAN

SHALOM	Hey, baby, peace. What's going on?
MAYIM	Just lookin' for my chakra, man. Tryin' to find my chakra.
SHALOM	That's groovy, man, I was trying to find my chakra too. But my old man's so uptight. He told me to get up and harvest the barley.
MAYIM	That's uncool.
SHALOM	Yeah, it's a bummer.
MAYIM	So, what are you gonna do?
SHALOM	Harvest the barley, I guess. Have to make some bread somehow.
MAYIM	I can dig it.
SHALOM	So I gotta beat it, but I wanted to clue you in about the happening at the well after Shabbat. There's gonna be havdala spices going around that'll blow your mind. Can you make the scene?
MAYIM	Far out! Oh, wait, man. My old lady said we're splittin' for Jerusalem after Shabbat. Gotta bring offerings to the Temple.
SHALOM	You going to the Temple? That's a drag. Those sellout kohaneem, man, they're piling up all that scratch and hangin' with the Seleucids. That's just not righteous, man.

MAYIM	I know! They're in fat city and fakin' Greek culture – it's grotty.
SHALOM	I'm hip, man. Know what I saw last time I went to Jerusalem? Jewish guys goin' to the gymnasium, and it's unreal what goes on there, ya dig?
MAYIM	I've heard stories. Dude, I'm not hung up but you gotta keep your clothes on when you're wrestling, man. I'm not into that crazy bunk the old heads are layin' down. I groove with God, not those funky squares on Mount Olympus.
SHALOM	It's their thing, and they can do what they wanna do, as long as I can keep doing *my* thing. Hey, who's the freak on the horse? He's coming over here.
MAYIM	Don't know that dude. Looks like kinda strung out. Hey, my brother! Peace.
JUDAH	Peace is just a dream, man. There's no peace until the people are free.
SHALOM	We're free, dude, we're laid back. All is mellow here.
JUDAH	So you're not hip to what went down in Modi'in.
MAYIM	No, we didn't hear anything about Modi'in, man. Lay it on me.
JUDAH	Dude, these Seleucids came to our commune, they were ready to rumble. I knew they get their kicks putting people down, but it got real heavy. My old man, Matityahu, he's the guru. He was about to light incense and start the chanting, when the Seleucid pigs rode up and just crashed it.
SHALOM	That's a downer. The fuzz got no right messin' with the Jews.

JUDAH   It wasn't the fuzz, man! These were actual pigs.

MAYIM   What did they do?

JUDAH   So some chickenhead Seleucid soldiers, man, they took one of these pigs and sacrificed it on the altar. The crowd tried to cut out, but the Seleucids made them stay, and said everyone had to *eat* some of the pig.

MAYIM   Gross!

JUDAH   Then the Jews tell the soldiers to eat dirt, man, and the soldiers whiff they're gonna bomb, so they grab one dude, put a sword to his throat, and yell, "Up against the wall, Jew!" It was a bad scene.

SHALOM   No way dude ate ham. That's <u>h</u>azzer, man. That's the worst. God's not down with that.

JUDAH   That was the bummer. He *did.*

SHALOM   Oh, man, he sold out? What a drag!

JUDAH   Yeah, and the crowd didn't know what to do, when my old man snaps out from transcendence and flips. He just goes ape. Dude grabs the sword and *offs the soldier.*

MAYIM   For real? Your old man did that?

JUDAH   Yeah, he just slays the Seleucid. Instant karma. Turns around to the crowd and waves the sword, and he says, "All who are for the Lord, follow me!"

MAYIM   I can't believe I wasn't hip to this.

SHALOM   We were at the beach all last week, man.

MAYIM   So what's down, dude? Your old man head for the hills?

JUDAH   He did, man, he's up at People's Park teaching tai chi. Everybody's there. He sent me back down here to bring you back.

SHALOM   Whoa, dude, that's not our kicks.

MAYIM   Yeah, we go with the flow. We live in the moment.

JUDAH   This *is* the moment. The Man's draggin' us down. It's time to do something, dude. Now it's on us to change the world.

SHALOM   Sounds like a hassle. Hell no, we won't go.

JUDAH   Look, dude, you want enlightenment?

MAYIM   Sure we want enlightenment.

JUDAH   The only path to enlightenment is through the Holy Temple in Jerusalem, man, and I heard that Seleucid establishment just palmed it. Now it's the Temple of Zeus, dude!

MAYIM   No way. Everybody says the Seleucids are drawing down.

JUDAH   That's a head trip, dude. There's more troops going over there, and more body bags coming back! You gotta question authority.

SHALOM   You sure you ain't buzzed, man?

JUDAH   I haven't touched it since that scene in Modi'in, man. That put me through some changes. I'm chill. Look, I need to score some swords and shields and get back to the hills. You gonna fight the power, or you gonna squat here and space out?

MAYIM   Shalom, dude's with it. We need to go see this guru. He sounds rad.

SHALOM   I'm down to rap with him, anyways.

                              ***

MATITYAHU   Welcome, my children. You bring the Divine essence to our circle.

JONATHAN   Right on.

MATITYAHU   I sense the spark of creation within you. As the spirit withdraws, the self expands to fill the universe with the One-ness of God.

MAYIM   *(in awe)* Heavy.

MATITYAHU   You must create your own path to truth, and to create it, you must first shatter your illusions.

SHALOM   What are the illusions, Master?

MATITYAHU   Greek idols are the illusions. Breathe in and prepare to transcend the Seleucid Empire. You'll need swords. Judah?

JUDAH   Here ya go.

MAYIM   Where will we find enlightenment?

MATITYAHU   In the Holy Temple in Jerusalem. But your spirit must first be purified; and the Temple, also, for it has been desecrated. If you seek union with the Boundless One, you must clear away all impediments. Starting with the statue of Zeus. Judah the Maccabeatnik will guide you on your path.

JONATHAN   Are you centered?

SHALOM   We're centered, baby. Let's do it.

***

MENELAUS   *(through bullhorn)* This is the High Priest! I repeat: this is the High Priest. By authority of King Antiochus of the Seleucid Empire, I order you to leave the premises immediately.

JONATHAN   The People's Campaign declines to disperse – pig!

MAYIM   Dude, it's not cool to drag down a kohayn.

JONATHAN   You're trippin', Mayim. Menelaus is *not* a kohayn. He paid off Antiochus to get the gig, and sold off the Temple vessels for the scratch.

MAYIM   Wait, was he the dude who put up that Zeus idol?

SHALOM   Like I said – unrighteous.

MENELAUS   *(through bullhorn)* Leave the Temple immediately, or you will be subject to arrest!

MAYIM   Those goons got billy-clubs, dude!

MENELAUS   *(through bullhorn)* Move in!

JONATHAN   Don't listen to the Terror through the wall, my people! It's our house! Go for it! Angel-headed hipsters, forward!

(There is general pandemonium as the Jews push their way into the Temple. Then silence.)

SHALOM   *(breathing heavily)* Oh, wow. Look at this place. It's so plastic.

MAYIM   The Temple is totaled. This is unreal. I'm so bummed out.

JONATHAN   We gotta lose these idols pronto. Oh, no, look! The eternal lava lamp!

MAYIM   It's empty. Oh, man, this is never supposed to go out.

SHALOM   Look around. Maybe there's some oil somewhere.

MAYIM   I'd buy some, but I'm tapped out.

SHALOM   Wait! The Hellenizers were hangin' here for years. Think! What's their bag?

JONATHAN   They're always wasted.

SHALOM   Dude! Look for pipes! There must be a stash

around somewhere.

MAYIM   They dropped some pipes here. You dreamin' there's enough resin to light the lava lamp? Power to you, man, but that's not happenin'.

SHALOM   Dig the lava lamp, Mayim. It's lighting up.

MAYIM   This is so cosmic!

JONATHAN   Go with the flow. Leave it to God, dude. Leave it to God.

In Which Pooh Meets a Maccabee

Alan Alexander Milne, some time before 1924, began telling imaginative stories to his young son Christopher Robin about his stuffed toys. In these tales, the toys came to life, and had all sorts of adventures that centered on the little boy. When the stories were published, they captured millions of hearts worldwide; Winnie-the-Pooh is still a beloved character a century later.

The naïve, simple title character struggles with his appetites and illusions. But he is a loyal, thoughtful, patient bear, and has taught countless children the virtue of friendship.

In a whimsical moment, I wondered how Pooh, Piglet, Eeyore and friends would cope with the disappearance of a favorite holiday. And I sent Christopher Robin to the rescue.

NARRATOR
CHRISTOPHER ROBIN
WINNIE-THE-POOH
EEYORE
RABBIT
PIGLET
OWL
TIGGER

NARRATOR   Once upon a time, a very long time ago now, about last Hanukkah, Winnie-the-Pooh lived in a forest all by himself under the name of Shaddai.

C. ROBIN   What does 'under the name' mean?

NARRATOR   It means there was a mezuza over his door that said "Shaddai" in gold letters. And he lived under it.

C. ROBIN   Winnie-the-Pooh wasn't quite sure.

POOH   Now I am.

NARRATOR   Then I will go on. One day, Pooh went out walking into the Hundred Acre Wood, and as he was walking, he was thinking. After some time of walking and thinking, and humming to himself, he found he was at the other side of the Hundred Acre Wood, and there he saw a stream burbling through a Boggy Place. And beside the stream was his friend, the old grey donkey, Eeyore.

POOH   Hullo, Eeyore.

EEYORE   Hullo, Pooh, I suppose.

POOH   Is something the matter, Eeyore? You look a little down in the dumps, and it's such a lovely, crisp winter's day.

EEYORE   If you say so. Today would be a lot lovelier with

candles and latkes. And presents.

POOH   That sounds a lot like – what day is today, Eeyore?

EEYORE   It's Hanukkah. Except it's been cancelled.

POOH   It's been cancelled?! But Hanukkah is my very favorite holiday!

EEYORE   Cancelled. Gloomy, but true. No more celebrations. No more gaity.

POOH   No chocolate coins all covered with foil? No more dreidels?

EEYORE   No more of that. It's an Official Pronouncement. Direct from Ty-Okus.

POOH   Ty-Okus does *not* sound like a very nice person!

EEYORE   I *was* rather looking forward to Hanukkah.

POOH   This is a very sad condition. I think we need to ask Christopher Robin. He'll know what to do.

EEYORE   Hopeless. But if you're going to see Christopher Robin, I may as well come along. Although there's nothing to be done about it.

NARRATOR So Eeyore and Pooh set out for Christopher Robin's house. As they passed through the Hundred Acre Wood, they came across Rabbit, who sat on a tree-stump with a Confused Look.

POOH   Hullo, Rabbit. How nice to find you here.

RABBIT   It's nice to find *you* here, too, Pooh. And Eeyore. As a matter of fact, it's nice to find *anyone* here, since I'm lost.

POOH   You're lost, Rabbit? But we're right here with you. If you're lost, then we're all lost, since we're in the Same Place. Where did you think you were going?

RABBIT

I *was* on my way to see Owl. But then I saw Piglet, and he was running round and round a tree, and he stopped to tell me that he was escaping from Ty-Okus.

EEYORE

Ty-Okus again. Pathetic, that's what it is.

POOH

It sounds like Piglet is a little Anxious. He's a Very Small Animal, you know, and -- did you say Ty-Okus?

RABBIT

Yes, that's what he said. He said Ty-Okus was trying to catch him.

POOH

This Ty-Okus – is he Fierce?

EEYORE

Very Fierce. And he doesn't like Hanukkah, either.

POOH

Would you happen to know if Ty-Okus is Fierce with Bears? Or just with Pigs?

RABBIT

Pigs, I have heard, are what Ty-Okus likes best.

EEYORE

I don't like to say it, but that sounds rather Ominous. First he cancels Hanukkah. Now he's chasing Piglet. It doesn't look good. Here today and gone to-morrow. After, all what's Hanukkah? Just a happy holiday. Not very important at all.

RABBIT

I've just remembered why I was going to Owl's house. I want him to write a sign for me, in very big letters. To say "Rabbit," so that Ty-Okus won't chase me too. Because Pigs are what Ty-Okus likes best.

NARRATOR

Just then, along came Christopher Robin, wearing a big helmet and carrying a wooden sword.

C. ROBIN

Hullo, everyone. What's up?

POOH

We were on our way to your house, Christopher Robin. There's a Horrible Ty-Okus somewhere, and he's cancelled the latkes and dreidels and candles, and he's bouncing at Piglet, and Eeyore's very sad indeed.

C. ROBIN   Well, I shall go and look at Ty-Okus. We mustn't let him bounce at Piglet, and we certainly won't give up Hanukkah. Come on!

NARRATOR   And so off they went – Christopher Robin, Winnie-the-Pooh, Rabbit and Eeyore. As they reached the top of the Forest, something small and pink came running down the path, and, plunk! bumped into Pooh.

PIGLET   Help, help! It's a terrible Ty-okus! It's a Tyabble Ter-Okus! Help! A Tokable Terrapus! Help, help, a tyacle Tokapus! Help! Oh, my goodness, Christopher Robin, I am *so* pleased to see you.

C. ROBIN   What's the matter, Piglet? Rabbit says that someone's chasing you.

PIGLET   Yes, it's a terrible Ty-Okus! It's an enormous, striped Ty-Okus and it Roars and it bounced at me so hard I fell into a gorse-bush.

POOH   Where did you see it, Piglet?

PIGLET   By the six pine trees near Owl's house.

C. ROBIN   Then that's where we must go.

NARRATOR   And so they all proceeded to Owl's house. Rabbit ran ahead and arrived first.

RABBIT   Owl! Are you home? You are Desperately Needed!

OWL   What's all this fuss? It looks like a Parade. Did I miss a holiday?

C. ROBIN   It's a holiday that's missing, Owl. Today is supposed to be Hanukkah, but Hanukkah's been cancelled by a Terrible Ty-Okus. And Piglet says it's bouncing around in a Careless and Dangerous Manner.

PIGLET   Who is very fond is Pigs. That's what I meant to talk to you about, Owl ...

EEYORE   It's an Official Pronouncement.

OWL   If you ask me...

EEYORE   I'm not asking you. I'm just telling everybody. There's no more Hanukkah, so just forget about dreidls and latkes and presents. It's Ty-Okus' fault, so Don't Blame Me.

OWL   This is serious indeed. Eeyore is Sad and Despondent, and Piglet is Very Anxious. Rabbit is Alarmed, and even Christopher Robin is Quite Concerned. Well! What shall we do?

RABBIT   It appears to me that the first order of business is to protect Piglet. As I have pointed out, Ty-Okus is very fond of Pigs. Which reminds me – Owl, could you write out a sign in very large letters that says "RABBIT"?

OWL   I believe I could do that with little difficulty. Allow me to go inside for a moment to obtain the necessary materials.

NARRATOR   A moment after Owl had gone inside his house, the others heard a rustling in the shrubs among the six pine trees. Suddenly, Tigger bounced into view.

TIGGER   Yoo-hoo! Why, hallo! Everybody's here!

PIGLET   There it is! The Tokable Terrapus! Oh, help! Help!

C. ROBIN   Is this what scared you, Piglet?

PIGLET   Yes, yes! Help!

NARRATOR   And Piglet hid behind Christopher Robin's wooden shield.

C. ROBIN   Tigger! It's only you.

TIGGER   It certainly is! It's all of me. Over here, over there. It's so much fun to be me!

C. ROBIN   Tigger, you've given Piglet at terrible fright. You bounced him into the gorse-bushes. And Rabbit is Anxious, and Eeyore is Despondent. Really, Tigger, you must be more careful of the feelings of Small Animals.

TIGGER   Oh! Did I? I didn't mean to. Piglet, I'm sorry. Rabbit, I'm sorry. Eeyore, I don't want you to be despondent. Especially when I'm so happy myself.

            Look at this parcel someone sent to me. It's a present! For me!

EEYORE   I'm sure that's very nice, Tigger, but you've caused Panic and Despair. It wasn't nice of you to cancel Hanukkah. Everyone was looking forward to it.

TIGGER   I did what? I don't remember doing that. Did I cancel Hanukkah?

EEYORE   You were distinctly heard shouting about it.

TIGGER   Cancel Hanukkah?

C. ROBIN   Tigger. What's in that parcel you have there?

TIGGER   It's a harmonica! That's why I'm so excited, Christopher Robin! It's a harmonica! And I've always wanted one! Look!

POOH   It's very nice, Tigger.

C. ROBIN   What did you say when you got this present, Tigger?

TIGGER   Well, I said, "A harmonica parcel!"

C. ROBIN	And what did you do after that?
TIGGER	I did what Tiggers do, of course. I bounced!
NARRATOR	And suddenly, everyone felt very foolish indeed.
C. ROBIN	Dear old Tigger. You see, everyone thought you said Hanukkah is cancelled.
TIGGER	Oh, no, no! I would never say that! That would be terrible! I love Hanukkah! In fact, this harmonica s a Hanukkah present. You can tell by the blue wrapping paper.
NARRATOR	Then Piglet said in a very small voice –
PIGLET	Is it safe to come out now?
C. ROBIN	Of course, Piglet. There isn't any Ty-Okus any more. It's just silly old Tigger.
PIGLET	Is he still bouncing?
RABBIT	He's not bouncing now.
NARRATOR	Just then, Owl came back with a pencil and paper.
OWL	Now, then, Rabbit, what was it you wanted me to write?
RABBIT	Thank you very kindly, Owl, but I don't think I need a sign anymore. I was going to carry a sign saying RABBIT, so the Ty-Okus wouldn't think I was a Pig. But maybe that wasn't a very nice thing to do to Piglet. And anyway, there isn't any Ty-Okus. It was only Tigger.
PIGLET	But he was very scary.
POOH	Tigger, although I'm a Bear of Very Little Brain, I feel sure that you should be more careful about all that bouncing.
OWL	One must recognize the sensibilities of Very Small

Animals, Tigger.

RABBIT   That's just what I say.

TIGGER   I'm sorry, everyone. I really didn't mean to scare anyone. I promise I'll be very careful when I bounce. And I didn't want to cancel Hanukkah!

              Everyone, it's all right. Hanukkah isn't cancelled.

RABBIT   Does that mean we can light some candles?

PIGLET   And spin some dreidels?

EEYORE   And eat some latkes?

C. ROBIN   Of course we will.

POOH   But, Christopher Robin, we don't have any of those things.

C. ROBIN   But *I* do, Pooh Bear. They're all at my house.

POOH   Are you quite sure about the latkes, Christopher Robin? Because I'm feeling a little rumbling in my tummy. I think it's time for a Little Something.

C. ROBIN   A little something with applesauce on it? Or sour cream?

POOH   Both, please!

OWL   That sounds like an excellent proposition.

TIGGER   Can I come along, too?

C. ROBIN   Of course, Tigger. Everybody can come.

EEYORE   Even me? If it's not too much trouble.

C. ROBIN   Eeyore, it wouldn't be Hanukkah without you.

EEYORE   I'm the soul of gaiety. Joke.

NARRATOR   And so everybody trouped in a great parade to

Christopher Robin's house. There were presents, and decorations, and candles, and lots and lots of good things to eat. So it was Hanukkah, as usual, just as it is every year. And everyone was very happy together.

Give Me Liberty or Give Me Death

— a revolutionary Hanukkah —

This vignette started out many years ago as a dialogue aimed at the Jewish children who are asked "Is Hanukkah the Jewish Christmas?" Always happy to assist, I articulated the real parallel to Hanukkah: America's Independence Day. It celebrated the unlikely victory of a relatively small band of freedom-fighters against a powerful imperial enemy. I think you can't find a closer parallel.

In neither case did newly-won independence produce an immediate utopia. However, the revolutionary ideals of both the Maccabees and the Americans remained strong in hearts and minds. In 1790, President Washington assured the Jews of Rhode Island that the young United States government gave to bigotry no sanction, and to persecution no assistance.

For that reason, I gave him a seat next to Judah Maccabee at an imaginary Great Generals Convention, and launched a conversation between them that explores their similar experiences.

MODERATOR
GEORGE WASHINGTON
JUDAH MACCABEE

(Both main characters are sitting at a table facing the audience. The MODERATOR stands at a lectern nearby.)

MODERATOR   This concludes the morning session of the Great Generals Convention; we'll break for lunch now. Please stroll through the booths in the Time Warp Ballroom, and enjoy the buffet. You can check your swords at the Courtesy Desk. We'll re-convene in one hour.

WASHINGTON   Well, I suppose I'll go check on the new line of hatchets. I'm sorry, I don't think we've met. My name's George Washington.

JUDAH   Judah Maccabee. *(They shake hands.)* Judean Army.

WASHINGTON   Continental Army.

JUDAH   Continental. I'm sorry, what continent would that be?

WASHINGTON   British North America. New World.

JUDAH   *New* world? Now that sounds intriguing.

WASHINGTON   Oh, it is! You missed it by ... let's see ... sixteen centuries, about.

JUDAH   British, you said. They're just a small tribe way up north of the Roman Empire.

WASHINGTON   They got some lucky breaks. So, if I'm remembering the Maccabean Wars from grammar school ... you were up against, was it the Greeks?

JUDAH   Close. It was the Seleucid Empire, one of Alexander the Great's spinoffs. The whole world was dominated by Greek culture, but it was only this

Assyrian emperor who weaponized it. It wouldn't be fair to pin the fault on the Greeks.

WASHINGTON The Greeks had a beautiful civilization. I learned Greek in school.

JUDAH Well, I don't share that view. My people were pretty traditional – still are – and Hellenism went way too far for us. Athletic competition in the *nude* – come on, now.

WASHINGTON I see your point.

JUDAH And their gods! Sleeping with each other's wives, turning each other into swans … Really. That's not religious leadership, as far as I'm concerned.

WASHINGTON There we agree completely.

JUDAH We would have co-existed, but then this maniac Antiochus IV ascended the throne. The Romans wouldn't let him have Egypt, so he got all petulant and decided to take it out on the Jews.

WASHINGTON Take it out – in what way?

JUDAH Well, we chased his puppet High Priest, Menelaus, out of Jerusalem, and he sent his soldiers to massacre every Jew they came across in the city. Women. Babies.

WASHINGTON A madman!

JUDAH Funny you should use that term. He called himself Antiochus Epiphanes. Had it stamped on coins.

WASHINGTON "Epiphanes"? God made manifest?

JUDAH Eee-yup. That's what he wanted people to call him. So, naturally, we decided to call him "Epimanes."

WASHINGTON Lunatic.

JUDAH   Exactly.

WASHINGTON I had no idea it was so bad. The British never would have considered such barbarity. Although they *did* have a mad king. But, still.

JUDAH   So it didn't end there. Antiochus felt moved to outlaw Jewish ritual observance, and installed a statue of Zeus in our Temple.

WASHINGTON I'd say that was a violation of an inalienable right. How many temples did you have?

JUDAH   Just the one! That's the thing! One Temple, one God, and furthermore, we never ever represent God in physical form!

WASHINGTON Ah. That's a slap in the face.

JUDAH   So, long story short, we rebelled.

WASHINGTON Freedom of religion is absolutely essential. We included it in our founding document.

JUDAH   What, freedom for *every* religion?

WASHINGTON Yes. Congress shall make no law respecting an establishment of religion, or prohibiting the free exercise thereof.

JUDAH   Wow. Mind blown. So, wait, don't you get a lot of really wacky religious nuts strutting around?

WASHINGTON Judah, you have no idea.

JUDAH   Okay, so, fill me in on this continent of yours, this British North America. And your war.

WASHINGTON All right. Europeans discovered the continent while looking for a sea route to Asia. The Spanish, English, French and Dutch all grabbed pieces of America – it actually turned out to be *two* continents – and most of the east coast of North America was British colonies by the 1700s. Then the philosophy of the natural rights of man, rule by the will of the people, took hold in the West, and since we didn't want to pay to support the empire, we declared independence.

JUDAH   The British taxed their colonies, then? Some things never change, do they?

WASHINGTON Yes. Our thirteen colonies confederated, and the fighting heated up. I was put in command of the Continental Army. Fortunately I had some military experience – I had been a major in the Virginia Regiment, helping the British fight the French.

JUDAH   Wait, you fought for the other side? The empire?

WASHINGTON Yes, I did. That was when we were all loyal Englishmen. Also I was a shareholder in the Ohio Company, whose interests we were defending against the French. And, you want to know something interesting – the British wouldn't give me a royal commission, even though I did really good work for them. If they had, I would have been a British officer and possibly have ended up fighting the American rebels.

JUDAH   Whoa! Big mistake by them, eh?

WASHINGTON As it turned out, yes. So, the war went on for eight years. There was infighting and very limited resources. Many of our soldiers were in rags, and the armaments were pathetic, at least till the French jumped in to help. Worse yet, many of the colonists didn't support the revolution. The Tories. They wanted to stay in the empire.

JUDAH   So they were like the Hellenists who didn't support our resistance.

WASHINGTON Maybe, except the Tories wanted to keep the status quo, while the Hellenists were the ones advocating change, right?

JUDAH   Huge change. The eradication of an ancient religion. Well, wait a minute, let me be fair. There were different degrees of Hellenists. Some just enjoyed Greek art and philosophy, while others enthusiastically helped the emperor's puppet High Priest rip the guts out of the Temple.

WASHINGTON   Nothing is simple, is it?

JUDAH   Nothing is simple. And to add to the mess, the Seleucids' army was pretty formidable and we had amateurs with dollar-store weapons and no discipline.

WASHINGTON   This is crazy! Same here! Farmer's boys armed with antique blunderbusses. The smart money was *not* on us, I can tell you that. Though as I mentioned, lucky for us the French hated the British and eventually pitched in.

JUDAH   No French reinforcements for us.

WASHINGTON   I guess not. But look – you won.

JUDAH   And you won. Two unlikely finales.

WASHINGTON   It was all about motivation.

JUDAH   Exactly. Exactly, it was motivation. Soldiers fight more valiantly for an ideal, for freedom, than they will ever fight for a salary.

WASHINGTON   Good thing too, as we didn't actually give them much by way of salary.

JUDAH   So it ended well? Things are still going strong in formerly-British America?

WASHINGTON   Some serious bumps along the way. But the founding document, the Constitution, still guides the nation, and our citizens are freer than most. You?

JUDAH   We had a hundred years of independence. Then, the Romans, and you know the rest. Israel only became a sovereign nation again recently. But, as you say, serious bumps.

WASHINGTON   Any regrets?

JUDAH   You know, I've thought a lot about that. In retrospect, we swung too hard the other way. My own family dynasty repressed dissidents to *our* practice. In fact, we were the only power in Jewish history that imposed conversions on non-Jews. We forced the Idumeans to convert, and one of them gave us King Herod. Not a good move, looking back on it. You?

WASHINGTON   I should *not* have invaded Canada. I dropped that brick, but good. They've been nice about it since, though. What about you, personally? Remembered? Forgotten?

JUDAH   Oh, remembered, definitely. I can't complain. Every Jewish kid still knows about the Maccabean war. They light a row of candles every year.

WASHINGTON   Candles? They light candles to remember a *war?*

JUDAH   Sure, why not? Well, there's a story about some oil miracle, but that was concocted years later to keep the Romans off our backs. What about America – you don't light candles?

WASHINGTON   *Americans* are not going to light *candles* to celebrate a *war victory*, Judah. We have fireworks.

JUDAH   Fire works?

WASHINGTON   Yes. Huge, brightly-colored explosions in the air. Loud. Americans like loud.

JUDAH   Oh. Okay. No, Hanukkah's not loud. We get loud on Purim, though.

WASHINGTON   That's the annual holiday – Hanukkah? I think I remember something about this. I was talking with some Jewish soldiers at Valley Forge.

JUDAH   What's Valley Forge?

WASHINGTON   It was a six-month encampment we spent training. And starving. Also dying of typhus and pneumonia. And it was winter, so the men were cold. It was bad. What was the worst time you had?

JUDAH   I suppose it was entering the Temple and seeing what the Assyrians had done to it. This Temple, you see, it was the soul of our people, our connection to God. And they had stolen it, turned it into a pagan temple. I felt as if my heart was ripped out. But, we purified it, we restored the vessels Antiochus stole, and we re-dedicated it. In some ways, that was tougher than the war. But we did it. It was like a miracle.

WASHINGTON   We have both witnessed miracles, Judah.

JUDAH   Yes. So Hanukkah celebrates that; do Americans have a commemorative day for victory?

WASHINGTON   We do, on the anniversary of our independence declaration. We don't have a name for it, just the date. Fourth day of July.

JUDAH   So more or less, it's the same as Hanukkah.

WASHINGTON   I'd say they're almost exactly the same. What do Jews do on Hanukkah?

JUDAH   Well, you know, the candles, fried potato pancakes … the dreidel game … and the American Jews are very big on Hanukkah presents.

WASHINGTON   We don't give Fourth of July presents.

JUDAH   What then?

WASHINGTON   We eat potato salad, and hot dogs ...

JUDAH   Oh my God.

WASHINGTON   And we play baseball.

JUDAH   Base ball? What's this?

WASHINGTON   Listen. There's a Little League game in the park across from the hotel. Come on outside. You'll like this.

A Charlie Brown Hanukkah

Charlie Brown has explained Christmas to children since 1965, when the animated TV special *A Charlie Brown Christmas* was first aired on CBS.

The title characters struggles with the demands of the cheerful holiday season, which he has trouble feeling; he sees only the excesses and the materialism. With the help of his sensible, humane friend Linus, Charlie Brown realizes the core meaning of the Christian holiday.

Since nearly every line of the script (and the music) is embedded in our memories, I thought the Peanuts gang could also help my character Isaac, who celebrates Hanukkah but feels drowned by the overwhelming Christmas festivities that dominate the season.

ISAAC
CHARLIE BROWN
LUCY
TEACHER
LINUS
SALLY
PIG-PEN

(Charlie Brown and Isaac are walking outside in the snow)

ISAAC   Charlie Brown, I think there must be something wrong with me. I feel like I'm getting everybody down. The Christmas spirit is everywhere, and it's like I don't exist. My family celebrates Hanukkah. We're invisible. I like getting presents, but I'm still not happy.

CHARLIE BROWN I always end up feeling depressed, too. I almost wish there weren't a holiday season. Just look at everybody – ice-skating, putting up decorations, sending greeting cards. I know nobody likes me – why do we need a special season to emphasize it?

ISAAC   Isn't that your dog's house?

CHARLIE BROWN Yes. Even he's gotten into the act. Lights and ornaments. Look, he's even hung up a stocking that says "gelt."

ISAAC   He's covering all his bases.

CHARLIE BROWN There's Lucy. At least *she's* not singing carols and baking cookies.

ISAAC   It looks like she's selling something at a booth.

CHARLIE BROWN Yes, she gives psychiatric advice. Why don't you go talk to her? It will only set you back five cents.

LUCY   All right, now, what seems to be the trouble? Before you begin, I must ask you to pay in advance. One cold, hard nickel. Mmm, how I love the smell of money! So, how can I be of service?

ISAAC   I feel annoyed. Everybody seems to be getting ready for Christmas, but it's not my holiday. I feel ignored and left out.

LUCY   Well, as they say, the mere fact that you realize you need help, indicates that you are not too far gone.

ISAAC   Actually, Lucy, my trouble is Christmas. I don't have anything *against* it, but it's everywhere. I can't get away from it. Every store window and every television commercial is selling Christmas. It's so hard to focus on Hanukkah.

LUCY   Are you afraid of Christmas? Maybe you have Clausophobia.

ISAAC   No, I like Christmas. It's pretty. The songs and the reindeer and the Christmas trees. Hanukkah can't compete with that. I feel marginalized.

LUCY   What you need is involvement. Maybe you should organize a Hanukkah tableau. With rabbis around a cradle, bringing gifts to baby Judah Maccabee. And animals standing around. I could be the Hanukkah Queen!

ISAAC   *(sighing)* No, Lucy. That's not what Hanukkah's all about. It's not a Jewish Christmas. You see, that's my whole problem.

LUCY   I know how you feel about all this Christmas business. I get depressed every year. I never get what I really want. Just toys, or a bike, or clothes.

ISAAC   What is it that you want, Lucy?

LUCY   Stock options.

(Charlie Brown and Isaac are sitting in class.)

ISAAC	It's no use trying, Charlie Brown. Even when you *do* find any Hanukkah around here, it's just a store trying to get you to buy more stuff. It's just like Christmas. Blatantly commercial.
TEACHER	Wah-wah-wahwahwahwah-wah-wah?
ISAAC	No, ma'am, you're not interrupting anything.
TEACHER	Wah-wah-wah?
ISAAC	I was just telling Charlie Brown about how hard it is to focus on Hanukkah when Christmas is everywhere.
TEACHER	Wah-wahwah-wahwah, wah wah?
ISAAC	Me? Tell the class about Hanukkah?
TEACHER	Wah, wahwahwah.
ISAAC	Uh, yes, okay, ma'am, I guess I can talk to the class about it tomorrow.

CHARLIE BROWN   Now you've done it.

LINUS	This isn't necessarily a bad thing, Charlie Brown. Sometimes when you organize your thoughts into a presentation, you're able to manage the situation better. I'm looking forward to Isaac's lesson tomorrow.
PIGPEN	I'll be happy to help, Isaac. I may not know a lot about Hanukkah, but I carry the dust of great past civilizations. Maybe the soil of ancient Babylon. Or even the sand of Solomon's Temple.
LUCY	You're an absolute mess, Pigpen. Just look at yourself.
PIGPEN	To the contrary. I didn't think I looked that good.

(Charlie Brown, Isaac, Linus and Sally are walking home from school)

SALLY   Maybe the class will understand Hanukkah if you present a dramatic exposition, Isaac. We could all be the characters in the Hanukkah story. There must be a part for someone with naturally curly hair.

ISAAC   That actually isn't a bad idea, Sally. The history of the Maccabee rebellion is pretty exciting.

CHARLIE BROWN   If you tell us about the Maccabees, we could put together a sort of skit. I bet nobody in the class knows anything about them.

LINUS   Who are the characters, Isaac?

ISAAC   Well, there's Judah Maccabee and his brothers. And the evil King Antiochus, and his Assyrian soldiers.

(They pass Snoopy on his doghouse)

CHARLIE BROWN   Are there any animals in the story?

ISAAC   I think the Assyrians used war-elephants in battle.

(Snoopy puffs himself up and trumpets like an elephant)

LINUS   So what happened?

(Piano music)

ISAAC   The Assyrian empire conquered the land of Judea. Everything was fine until King Antiochus decided to impose Greek culture on the land. He outlawed the Jewish religion and forced the Jews to worship pagan idols. Judah Maccabee formed an army of guerilla fighters and beat the Assyrians all the way back to Jerusalem. They reclaimed the Holy Temple from the pagans, and rededicated it to God.

(Music stops)

PIGPEN   That doesn't sound anything like the Christmas story, Isaac.

ISAAC   It *isn't* anything like the Christmas story, Pigpen.

SALLY   Then why are Christmas and Hanukkah at the same time?

ISAAC   It's an accident of the calendar.

SALLY   But they both have lights and presents.

CHARLIE BROWN It's a dark time of year, so lights make sense.

PIGPEN   And if everyone else is getting presents, why not the Jewish kids?

LINUS   Hanukkah and Christmas present an interesting challenge. You have to maintain your distinctiveness, while participating fully in the wider culture.

ISAAC   That's sort of like the Maccabees' problem. They were living in the Assyrian empire, but they didn't want the Assyrians' religion. They wanted the Jewish people to survive.

LINUS   You would think that would solve the problem, right? But now Christmas outplays Hanukkah. A lot of people don't know anything about Hanukkah or why some people celebrate it.

CHARLIE BROWN Back then, the Jewish people were up against a murderous enemy that hated them. But now, you're fully integrated into society. You're free to express your heritage however you like.

ISAAC   But it's useless, Charlie Brown. Linus is right. We're allowed to celebrate being Jewish, but Christmas is so big that it eclipses everything else.

LINUS   I don't think it's so hopeless, Isaac. You have to start somewhere. Tomorrow you'll tell the class all about Hanukkah, and we'll help you. What do you need us to bring?

ISAAC   Well … I guess we'll have to have a Hanukkah me-
                 norah, some latkes, and a dreidel.   And some
                 chariots, swords, shields, and a pagan idol.

PIGPEN   I'll look in my garage.

ISAAC   Thanks, Pigpen.

(Snoopy is decorating his doghouse)

ISAAC   What's your dog up to, Charlie Brown?

CHARLIE BROWN Snoopy, what are you dressed as?

(Charlie Brown sees a sign in front of the doghouse that says, "Have Your Picture Taken With Hanukkah Harry.")

                 That's my dog, all right. Misappropriating cultural
                 icons to make money.

(Snoopy brings out a menorah covered with tinsel and ornaments.)

CHARLIE BROWN Rats. Sorry about this, Isaac.

ISAAC   That's okay, Charlie Brown.   I'm starting to get
                 used to it.

(Isaac is standing in front of the class)

TEACHER   Wah wah wah-wah, wahwah.

ISAAC   Thank you, ma'am. The important thing to know
                 about Hanukkah is, it's not really anything like
                 Christmas. Hanukkah celebrates history's first war
                 for religious freedom. In 165 BCE, Jewish practices
                 had been outlawed. The Assyrians wanted their
                 subjects to worship the Greek gods. So the Jews
                 rebelled against the Assyrian empire. Led by Judah
                 the Maccabee, they defeated a powerful army. The
                 Maccabees, ruled Judea for a hundred years before
                 the land was conquered once again, by the Romans.

SALLY   What about the oil? Wasn't there oil that lasted for eight days?

ISAAC   It's true that the menorah in the Temple was supposed to stay lit all the time. There was a legend that the Maccabees found just a small amount of sacred oil, only enough for one day. But it miraculously lasted eight days, long enough to prepare some more.

LUCY   I've heard of this Judah Maccabee. Everybody talks about how great he was. Judah Maccabee wasn't so great.

ISAAC   What do you mean, Judah Maccabee wasn't so great?

LUCY   He never got his picture on bubble-gum cards, did he? Have you ever seen his picture on a bubble-gum card? Hmmm? How can you say someone's great who's never had his picture on bubble-gum cards?

CHARLIE BROWN   Good grief.

TEACHER   Wah wah-wah-wah.

ISAAC   Today we celebrate by lighting the Hanukkah menorah, singing holiday songs, eating latkes and jelly doughnuts, and playing the dreidel game. Since Hanukkah happens around Christmas time, a lot of us get presents too.

PIGPEN   Don't you miss having a Christmas tree, Isaac?

ISAAC   Christmas trees are really nice, but we have our sukkah to decorate in the fall. We also have carnivals and costumes on Purim, a treasure hunt on Passover, and a picnic on Lag B'Omer. So I don't think we're actually deprived.

LINUS   Would you say that Hanukkah is a season of peace, like Christmas, Isaac?

ISAAC   Well, Hanukkah celebrates a military victory. So it's not a holiday of peace. Our holiday of peace is every week, on Shabbat.

LUCY   But what about everything else? Santa Claus and reindeer and the carol service and everything? I can't imagine not having those.

ISAAC   Those are beautiful, too, Lucy. But it's like birthdays. You have yours, and it's fun to come to your party and celebrate with you. But it's still not *my* birthday. That's another celebration, and it's different, because it's mine. And I want you to celebrate it with me, too.

SALLY   That makes perfect sense, Isaac.

CHARLIE BROWN   I don't think we'd all want to have the same birthday.

ISAAC   It just wouldn't be as much fun.

CHARLIE BROWN   Happy Hanukkah, Isaac.

ISAAC   Merry Christmas, Charlie Brown.

Don't Let Your Dreidel Go Down

— a Hanukkah bluegrass jam —

It's really an interesting phenomenon. Bluegrass music, a genre that is firmly rooted in the American southern gospel tradition, attracts Jews.

It certainly attracts me – I can't get enough of it. My husband plays bluegrass banjo. Whenever we go to concerts, jams, or festivals, a huge number of the audience is Jewish. And a lot of the performers are, too: David Grisman, Andy Statman, Eric Weissberg, Steve Mandell, Bob Yellin, Margot Leverett, Roger Sprung, and legions of others known better to their local communities. The connection is so strong that some dubbed the genre "Jewgrass."

What drew Jews to this music? The site of its northern mecca during the 1950's and '60's – Manhattan's Washington Square Park on Sunday afternoons – is one explanation. No doubt, there are others. I'll leave it to music historians to explore all of the reasons why, and focus my energies on presenting here a handful of bluegrass classics re-written to tell the story of Hanukkah. This isn't a script so much as a collection of song paradies. Chord progressions are included.

EMCEE   Welcome one and all to our Hanukkah hootenanny! We're here to tell the story of those old-time Maccabees and have a real good time. Let's kick things off with that bluegrass favorite, *The Old Menorah.*

THE OLD MENORAH (Melody: "The Midnight Special")

I / I / I / IV
IV / IV / IV / I
I / I / I / V
V / V / V / I

Well, you come home in the evenin'
Like every working man
You see the dreidls on the table
You smell the latkes in the pan

You open presents if you got 'em
You see the candles glow
You think about the Hasmoneans
And what they did so long ago

> Oh let that old menorah
> Shine her light on me.
> Let that old menorah
> Shine her ever-lovin' light on me.

When they come into the temple
They seen the way it was
Since it was good and desecrated
They did what Maccabees does.

Well they broke up all the idols
They fixed the altar up right
And a jar of olive oil
Sure made the light shine bright

> Oh let that old menorah
> Shine her light on me.
> Let that old menorah

Shine her ever-lovin' light on me

EMCEE   Didn't that sound real good? I love that old time
               religion. Now we're gonna slow things down just a
               little bit and tell the story about how all the trouble
               started, way back in the days of the Seleucid Em-
               pire.

ANTIOCHUS (Melody: "Fox on the Run")

Chorus:
I / V / ii / IV
ii / V / IV / I
I / V / ii / IV
ii / V / IV / I
IV / IV / IV / I

Verse:
IV / I / V / I
IV / I / II / V
IV / I / V / I
IV / I / V / I

He walked in the door and he stood at the altar
And he planned to complete the disgrace he'd begun
A statue of Zeus and a hog for the slaughter
Our Temple defiled by the time he was done.
    By the time, by the time, by the time, he was done.

Everybody knows what Antiochus did
When Judea was brought down by the evil Seleucid
He robbed 'em and despoiled 'em, and like a Philistine
Profaned the sacred Temple with the blood of a swine.
    With the blood, with the blood, with the blood of a swine.

He walked in the door and he stood at the altar
And he planned to complete the disgrace he'd begun
A statue of Zeus and a hog for the slaughter
Our Temple defiled by the time he was done.
    By the time, by the time, by the time, he was done.

EMCEE   But old Antiochus didn't know who he was
             messin' with, did he? Ol' Matityahu got good and
             riled up when he heard about it!

MATITYAHU   (Melody: "Darling Cory")

I / I / I / I
I / I / V / V
I / I / I / I
I / I / V / I

Wake up, wake up, Matityahu,
What makes you sleep so sound?
Antiochus' army is a-coming
For to tear Judea down.

Matityahu he struck down the idol
And when he saw those soldiers flee
He called to the Jews all around him
"If you're for the Lord, follow me!"

Well, the first time I seen Matityahu
He was with his rebel band
Had a yamulka strapped to his forehead
And a broadsword in his hand.

And he told his young son Judah,
'You're gonna set our people free.
And because you strike like a hammer,
We'll call you the Maccabee.'

Dig a hole, dig a hole in the meadow
Dig a hole in the cold, cold plains
And remember Matityahu
For his blood runs in your veins.

EMCEEE   So the battle was on. That little band of freedom
             fighters trained in the hills and then came after the
             empire's soldiers. They had the Lord on their side!

TEMPLE BLUES (Melody: "White House Blues")

I / I / I / I
IV / IV / IV / I
I / V / I / I

Antiochus plundered God's holy hall
Judah said, rascal, you're bound for a fall
It's time to go, it's time to go.

Antiochus told him, we'll fight man to man
The Maccabee answered, we'll beat you if we can
And send you home, and send you home.

Look here, you rascal, you see what you've done
You stole our temple vessels, you son of a gun
Now get on home, now get on home.

They fought with the spear and they fought with the sword
The Jews won the day in the name of the Lord
So they were free, so they were free.

EMCEE   The battle for Jerusalem was won, and the Holy
                Temple was purified and re-dedicated. But the
                eternal light had gone out, and it would take eight
                long days to prepare the oil to light it again. Only a
                small bottle was found. It could never last eight
                daus – unless there was a miracle.

IT TAKES A LOT OF OIL (Melody: "It Takes a Worried Man")

I / I / I / I
IV / IV / IV / I
I / I / I / I
V / V / I / I

I went up to the Temple, to see just what they done
I went up to the Temple, to see just what they done
I went up to the Temple, to see just what they done.
That olive oil -- we ain't got hardly none.

It takes a lot of oil, to light the Ner Tamid
It takes a lot of oil, to light the Ner Tamid
It takes a lot of oil, to light the Ner Tamid
A big old barrel, that's 'bout how much we need.

Twenty-one soldiers of Judah Maccabee (3x)
And every soldier, he fought for liberty.

It takes a lot of oil, to light the Ner Tamid ...

One little ol' jar, will last for just one day (3)
That kohayn said, let's light that lamp and pray

It takes a lot of oil, to light the Ner Tamid ...

Looked high and low, for oil to light that light
And eight days later, the lamp's still burnin' bright.

It takes a lot of oil, to light the Ner Tamid (3x)
Turns out one jar, was all that lamp did need.

If anybody ask you, "Well who made up this song?" (3x)
Tell 'em 'twas me, and I done been here and gone.

It takes a lot of oil, to light the Ner Tamid (3x)
Turns out one jar, was all that lamp did need.

EMCEE   What a wonderful story those Maccabees left us.
               We are so blessed with our inheritance.   My
               friends, I can smell those wonderful latkes our Sis-
               terhood is cooking up, and I know you're just as
               ready as I am to tuck those in, so let's end with that
               old favorite, *This Little Light of Mine*.

THIS LITTLE LIGHT OF MINE

I / I / I / I
IV / IV / IV / I
I / I / III / vi
I / V / I / I

This little light of mine, shines in the holy shrine (3x)
　　Let it shine, let it shine, let it shine!

Just like the Torah, it lights up that menorah (3x)
　　Let it shine, let it shine, let it shine!

All through the darkness, I'm gonna let it shine (3x)
　　Let it shine, let it shine, let it shine!

The Swejhis of Qumar

– a West Wing Hanukkah –

The West Wing was a beloved television series, created by Aaron Sorkin, that was broadcast on NBC from 1999 to 2006. It was a fantasy of a humane, morally clear Presidential administration, and it got many of us through some difficult years. I know lots of people who can still recite lengthy passages from the script.

The Jewish characters included communications director Toby Ziegler, and deputy chief of staff, Josh Lyman. They frequently referred to our traditions, personalities, texts, and issues, which I imagine are important to Mr. Sorkin. Devotees were proud.

A number of episodes were set in holiday times, mainly Thanksgiving and Christmas. Here's a short script I'm sneaking in for Hanukkah.

PRESIDENT JOSIAH BARTLET
CHARLIE YOUNG, PERSONAL AIDE TO THE PRESIDENT
LEO MCGARRY, CHIEF OF STAFF
TOBY ZIEGLER, COMMUNICATIONS DIRECTOR
JOSH LYMAN, DEPUTY CHIEF OF STAFF
DONNA MOSS, JOSH'S ASSISTANT
CJ CREGG, PRESS SECRETARY

(The Oval Office. Charlie Young is sorting a pile of notes. President enters.)

PRESIDENT   Lost causes, Charlie. The theme of the day is, lost causes.

CHARLIE   Good morning, Mr. President.

PRESIDENT   Which I seriously doubt, but I appreciate your optimism.

CHARLIE   Anything I can do to help, Mr. President?

PRESIDENT   If you can find a sedative that the Sultan of Qumar and his family might enjoy for a year or two, that would be very helpful.

CHARLIE   I'll look around, sir.

(Leo MacGarry enters)

LEO   Good morning, Mr. President. I assume you read the briefing on the insurgency.

PRESIDENT   I did, and I'm fully convinced that history isn't linear after all; it's on an eternal, repeating loop. The Joint Chiefs meet at two. *(Shouts)* Mrs. Landingham, if you would ask Josh to come in as soon as he's finished his report.

LEO   It looks like the Swejhi troops mean business.

PRESIDENT   They think they have God on their side. Don't we all?

(Toby enters)

TOBY Mr. President.

PRESIDENT Toby! You look seasonally festive.

TOBY I'm eternally festive, sir.

PRESIDENT What's new in the great world?

TOBY Mr. President, CNN and C-SPAN plan to carry your holiday message live, so I thought maybe you'd want some prepared remarks. For a change. Sir.

PRESIDENT Do I infer that last year's exposition on historical eschatology didn't meet your standards, Toby?

TOBY It was – academically sound, I'm sure, sir. But the networks switched away after –

PRESIDENT After twenty-three seconds.

TOBY Yes, sir. After twenty-three seconds, switched to a segment about multi-cultural snowmen –

PRESIDENT That's important too.

TOBY Yes, sir.

PRESIDENT Well, go ahead, Toby, you know your business. This is when?

TOBY Eleven o'clock. Thank you, Mr. President.

PRESIDENT What's next?

(Toby exits. Josh enters)

LEO Josh, the President wants everyone to be seasonally festive.

JOSH   Mr. President, I have a dreidel in my pocket and
                I'm ready for all challengers.

PRESIDENT   Good! That's what we like to hear. Tell me about
                the insurgents.

JOSH   The Swejhi community has lived in the hills of
                western Qumar for over a thousand years. They
                were an independent confederation of tribes for
                most of that time. They practice a monotheistic re-
                ligion and they resist any corruption of their ritual
                system. Recently the Qumari government has
                cracked down on Swejhi religious practice, outlaw-
                ing its festivals and life cycle ceremonies. There
                have been executions of resisters. Three months
                ago, Qumari troops took over the Swejhis' central
                sanctuary, looted its valuables and converted it to a
                government mosque.

PRESIDENT   This seems to happen like clockwork in that part of
                the world. Still, you don't like to see our strategic
                allies behaving like this. It's bad press.

JOSH   The Swejhis organized a guerilla force late last year
                and they've been hammering at army bases all over
                the western hills. The insurgents don't seem to
                have any outside support, just local tribespeople.
                They've taken control of most of their historic terri-
                tory, and their intent seems to be to re-take the
                sanctuary.

LEO   What's our ambassador saying?

JOSH   He's not sure which way this is going, and advises
                us to hold back on any public statements.

PRESIDENT   What about our Qumari airbase?

JOSH   They're on high alert. Mr. President, the reports of
                atrocities against the rebels are pretty disturbing.

PRESIDENT   What are the Swejhis demanding?

JOSH   Up till recently, they've been asking for religious freedom. But since the sanctuary takeover, they're not looking for compromise. Now they're talking about complete independence.

LEO   This reminds me of something, I can't remember what.

PRESIDENT   Sounds like George Washington and the Continental Army.

JOSH   Maybe that's it.

PRESIDENT   I'm meeting with the brass at two. Let's see what our satellites are showing, and then I'll call Abdul Shareef.

JOSH   Thank you, Mr. President.

(Josh exits the Oval Office. Donna falls in with him as he walks down the hallway.)

DONNA   We have the National Girl Scout Choir in the Mural Room at eleven.

JOSH   Are they bringing cookies?

DONNA   Didn't you say a different group was in the Mural Room then?

JOSH   I thought it was the New England Klezmer Conservatory Band.

DONNA   *(excited)* The New England Klezmer Conservatory Band!? I *love* them! With Hankus Netsky? They're the greatest!

JOSH   They make me think I'm at my great-grandmother's wedding.

DONNA   Great art is eternal, Josh.

JOSH   We should have them perform with the Girl Scouts.

I hear the girls can earn a badge for Yiddish theater music.

DONNA   I still have mine.

(CJ appears in Josh's office doorway.)

CJ   Josh, Danny says you've invited the entire press corps to the menorah-lighting. Is this true?

JOSH   Technically, it's a hanukkiah-lighting. A menorah only has seven --

CJ   Josh, traditionally that's an event for Jewish leadership to attend. If you invite four dozen reporters, there won't be enough room for any Jewish leadership.

JOSH   It's just a polite gesture, CJ. The reporters aren't going to come. They light their own hanukkiot at home.

CJ   Possibly some of them do, but I don't think I've heard the answer to my question, Josh. Did you –

JOSH   Why is this important?

CJ   It's a chain-of-command issue, Josh. You need to take responsibility for your decisions. It's a matter of character and maturity. Did you invite the press corps or not?

JOSH   Sam did.

CJ   Okay. Oh! Mr. President.

(President arrives outside Josh's office door.)

PRESIDENT   I thought I overheard a discussion about lighting the hanukkiah.

JOSH   Yes.

PRESIDENT   You know, two thousand years ago, there was a

disagreement between the two great academies of Jewish law, Beit Shammai and Beit Hillel, about how to light the Hanukkah lights. Want me to tell you about it?

CJ   *(feeling resigned)* Oh, would you?

PRESIDENT   Beit Shammai advocated lighting all eight lights on the first night of Hanukkah, to indicate the maximum potential of the commandment. Countering Shammai, Beit Hillel held that the focus should be on the increasing power of the miracle, and that one light should be lit on the first night, two on the second, et cetera.

CJ   And what was decided?

PRESIDENT   Beit Hillel's view prevailed.

DONNA   Why?

JOSH   Probably had something to do with the Temple press gaggle and the Sanhedrin news cycle.

CJ   How did Shammai take the decision?

PRESIDENT   There's no record of his reaction, but Shammai was notoriously impatient and bad-tempered.

JOSH   Whereas you, Mr. President, are *never* ill-tempered.

PRESIDENT   Are you sassing me, Josh?

JOSH   No, sir.

PRESIDENT   Good. A lack of civility in public discourse is unpardonable.

DONNA   You pardon turkeys.

PRESIDENT   Turkeys taste better. Charlie! Time for the Mural Room?

CHARLIE   The klezmer band is set up, the Smithsonian sent a menorah, and the Girl Scouts are listening to a rabbi.

PRESIDENT   We better get in there quick.

CHARLIE   Yes, sir.

(Charlie, President, CJ, Donna and Josh start walking down a hallway. Leo catches up)

LEO   Mr. President, the National Security Advisor says the Swejhi insurgents have taken the central sanctuary. The Qumari troops have retreated.

PRESIDENT   What business did the troops have in there, anyway?

(Toby joins them as they walk.)

LEO   The Qumari ambassador is calling on us to condemn the insurgency.

TOBY   Do you want my opinion?

PRESIDENT   I have a feeling I'm going to get it.

TOBY   The Swejhi aren't waging a war of aggression. All they want is to practice their religion. The Qumari threw the first punch, and if they're getting spanked by a bunch of dudes with pop-guns, they were asking for it.

PRESIDENT   And those Qumari oil fields that fuel 30% of our economy?

TOBY   Oil fields be damned, sir.

PRESIDENT   We'll see how that turns out. Have the speech?

TOBY   Right here, sir.

(They enter the Mural Room)

PRESIDENT   Hello, klezmorim! Hello, Rabbi! Hello, Girl Scouts, did you bring any cookies?

CJ   They brought eighty-five boxes of cookies, and those have been sent to the residence, Mr. President.

PRESIDENT   Excellent! Welcome, leaders of the Jewish community, to the White House. Now, I don't mean to put a damper on this event, but before we light this hanukkiah and let Mr. Netsky strike up the band, I have a few remarks.

(He begins to read Toby's speech.)

For many Americans, this is the season of peace and gratitude. The harvest has been brought in, and the lights we kindle to illuminate the long, dark nights remind us to share our blessings with the homeless, the hungry, and the shut-in. In this season of generosity, let's give thanks for our troops and our veterans who have sacrificed – who have sacrificed so much –

(He pauses, passes the speech back to Toby, and puts his hands in his pockets.)

Peace is in our songs and on our greeting cards. We hope – we pray – that our faith leads us on paths of peace. But there are times when men must take up arms because they love peace. If our nation had marched to stop Hitler when he marched into Czechoslovakia, the world would have been at peace long before 1945. We've heard this story before, with different names, in different places. In fact, it's happening right now, in Qumar. Sometimes we must take up arms when diplomacy fails.

The Maccabees of old fought their oppressors when they had no choice. They rebelled against a mighty empire and won the first war for freedom of religion. They won because their ancient heritage was too precious to lose.

The lamp those Maccabees lit in their sanctuary still shines. We remember what those guerilla fighters in the Judean hills left us: the knowledge that faith is ultimately a greater power than savagery.

We thank God for the miracles, for the redemption, for the valorous deeds, and for the salvation which you wrought for our ancestors in those days, at this time of year.

(The New England Klezmer Conservatory Band plays a lively version of "Al Ha-Nisim" as the camera closes in on the hand of the rabbi lighting the first candle.)

Captain's Log - Stardate: Kislev, 25

– a Star Trek Hanukkah –

As you know, *Star Trek* is Gene Roddenberry's science fiction television series launched in 1966. The original series lasted four years, to be followed by other generations both live-action and animated. Even if you didn't watch it, you probably know what Klingons and tribbles are, and could salute Mr. Spock if requested.

The starship Enterprise is a vessel of the United Federation of Planets, sent to explore new worlds and, significantly, to provide diplomacy to places torn by conflict. Hanukkah is the story of a conflict, and transplanting it to another planet isn't so hard. So I did.

It helps that the two main characters of the original series, Captain Kirk and Mr. Spock, were played by Jewish actors. William Shatner explained that, in science fiction, people are looking for answers, and the genre tries to explain the inexplicable – just as religion does. And Leonard Nimoy, z"l, contributed the gesture of greeting that originated with ancient Jewish priests, or *kohaneem* – the split-finger blessing signal.

In this script, the greedy and wicked Seleugon empire is attacking the Vulsid society, which must consider an uneasy alliance with their Hellerite brothers, whom they resent for their perceived faithlessness to ancient tradition.

CAPTAIN JAMES T. KIRK
FIRST OFFICER SPOCK
CHIEF MEDICAL OFFICER LEONARD MCCOY
COMMUNICATIONS OFFICER NYOTA UHURA
MATTATHIAS, KOHAYN OF THE VULSIDS
ARISTEAS, A HELLERITE JUDEAN
JUDAS, SON OF MATTATHIAS
DEMETRIUS, LIBRARIAN OF ALEXANDRIA
EPIPHANES, SELEUGON EMPEROR

KIRK   Space – the final frontier. These are the voyages of
                the starship Enterprise. Its five-year mission: to
                explore strange new worlds. To seek out new life
                and new civilizations. To boldly go where no one
                has gone before.

(On the bridge)

KIRK   Captain's log, star date 3596.12. The Enterprise is
                navigating toward Acra 168 in the Mesopotamian
                star cluster. Our purpose is to establish diplomatic
                channels between hostile factions on the planet,
                and to prevent escalation of the tensions, if possi-
                ble. Mr. Spock, a full analysis of sensor readings.

SPOCK   Acra is one of the few star clusters classified as
                Continual Reduplicaton galaxies. It occupies a spe-
                cialized time continuum wherein history keeps re-
                peating itself.

MCCOY   If the same things keep happening again and again,
                why bother with diplomacy?

SPOCK   Because if its historical trajectory can be re-set in a
                more peaceful and productive pattern, that new
                history will become the one that is repeated. In
                other words, if innocent lives can be saved one
                time, others will be saved an infinite number of
                times in the future.

KIRK   It sounds too bizarre to be true.

SPOCK   One could argue that time, not space, is the final frontier.

KIRK   In any case, Starfleet Command instructs us to respond to a distress signal from Commander Mattathias from the Vulsid community, which is under attack by the Seleugon Empire. The Seleugons have unsuccessfully attempted to invade planet Masr, and they now may be seeking a softer target to colonize and exploit. Mr. Spock, what do you know about the Vulsids?

SPOCK   Captain, the Vulsids are a relatively small community that has lived on the planet for over a thousand of your earth-years. They are devoted to the service of a monotheistic deity and live according to a revered scripture and careful interpretation of it. One faction of this community is the Hellerites, who share the same traditions but have also absorbed the culture of the Alexandrians who also inhabit the planet.

MCCOY   So who are the Seleugons attacking?

SPOCK   So far, the sensor is reading a Seleugon assault on both the Hellerites and the Vulsids; but, even so, these two communities are still having difficulties finding common cause. Captain, I must inform you of a personal connection to this situation. I, myself, am half Vulsid. My father descends from these people.

KIRK   Spock, I expect that you won't allow your personal feelings to affect our mission here.

SPOCK   That's not likely, Captain.

KIRK   Lieutenant Uhura, encode a transmission to the Vulsid command center. Ask them if they would come aboard the Enterprise for a conference with a

Hellerite delegation, with us as intermediaries. Encode the same message to the Hellerites.

UHURA   Yes, Captain.

KIRK   The Seleugon fleet is in this quadrant. Their emperor is known to be hostile and now is even more, shall we say, cantankerous after losing planet Masr. It's not likely that he'll be in a mood to negotiate peace. Mr. Sulu, have the crews stand by photon torpedo positions.

SPOCK   Captain, my tricorder suggests that the Seleugons have already established sleeper cells on Acra. One of their agents, Menelaus, has been installed within the Hellerite community as their Great Kohayn, and is feeding information and resources to the Emperor Epiphanes. The Hellerites have been unable to dislodge Menelaus, and their frustration is growing.

KIRK   Maybe that's what they need to cement an alliance with the Vulsids.

UHURA   Captain, the Hellerites are preparing to send a shuttlecraft with two of their diplomats. Permission to board on their arrival?

KIRK   Permission granted. Any response from the Vulsids?

UHURA   Yes, sir. Their Kohayn and his son are en route to the Enterprise.

(Conference room.   Spock, Kirk, McCoy, Aristeas, Demetrius, Mattathias and Judas.)

KIRK   Gentlemen, welcome aboard the Enterprise. I understand you have not met personally until now. Mattathias, Great Kohayn of the Vulsids, and his son Judas. Aristeas of the Hellerite community in Alexandria, and his colleague Demetrius, librarian of Alexandria.

(The diplomats bow to each other, Mattathias rather coldly.)

MCCOY   The Federation hopes that your two factions will be willing to work together to resist the incursion of Emperor Epiphanes' forces into Acra.

MATTATHIAS   The Hellerites have already permitted a Seleugon incursion.

ARISTEAS   If you are speaking of the ascension of Menelaus ...

MATTATHIAS   Permitting him the holy office of the Great Kohayn is only one outrage.

ARISTEAS   It could not be helped. Menelaus came to Acra guarded by armed legions of Seleugons.

JUDAS   And Menelaus paid for the escort personally, with riches stolen from our treasury.

KIRK   Gentlemen, there appears to be little choice. Epiphanes' forces are inestimable. Separately, you have no hope of resisting them. Together, you might have a chance. And without a directive from the Federation, I am unable to intervene.

MATTATHIAS   We are forbidden to take common cause with the Hellerites, who have polluted our sacred traditions with foreign practices.

DEMETRIUS   Polluted, Great Kohayn? Aren't you being rather harsh? The Hellas people of Alexandria are happy to exchange wisdom and art with the Judeans of Acra. We each have profound and beautiful philosophies; why not share them so each can grow?

JUDAS   You who are not of our lineage cannot understand why our culture must be protected.

ARISTEAS   Your argument is selective, Judas. Does not the book of Solomon, which you revere, make use of

Hellenic ideas? Does it not define wisdom just as they define reason? The same concept, but with different names?

MATTATHIAS   If it were only that, we'd have no quarrel. Poems, dramas and debates do not offend us. But their adoration of a pantheon of amoral gods – this, to us, is anathema.

DEMETRIUS   There, you have used a Hellerite word to represent your view.

MATTATHIAS   Words are nothing. But your deeds cannot be tolerated. You celebrate the human body without any modesty – without, even, any clothing! You represent your gods with statues, while the true God is unknowable, without physical attributes. We celebrate personal discipline – while you Hellerites revel in hedonism.

ARISTEAS   Those of us in the Hellerite community reject those excesses, but treasure the pursuit of knowledge that both the Vulsids and the Alexandrians share.

JUDAS   Knowledge that you cannot even discuss in your ancestral tongue, which you have forgotten!

SPOCK   I find it fascinating that this philosophic argument takes precedence over the existential threat that faces you.

KIRK   Gentlemen! I have seen what the Seleugons do to planets like yours. They pillage all the resources they wish to take, and erase any memory of the cultures they conquer. While I appreciate your dedication to rhetorical discussion, your situation is urgent. You can't afford the luxury of philosophical bickering!

(Kirk's wrist communicator blinks.)

KIRK   Yes, Lieutenant Uhura?

UHURA   Captain, the Seleugon Emperor is initiating contact. Shall I transmit the frequency to the reception screen?

KIRK   Yes, Lieutenant.

(Epiphanes' face materializes on the screen.)

EPIPHANES   Captain Kirk. I am informed that you confer with representatives of the target Judean society. I wish to convey my final warning to them.

KIRK   Emperor, if you choose to attack the population of a peaceful planet, the Federation will be forced to take military measures to protect them.

EPIPHANES   What the Federation chooses to do is of no concern to me. The Judeans have refused to submit to our offer of terms, and we will commence engagement.

KIRK   Your terms? What are they?

EPIPHANES   An immediate end to their traditional practices, and the institution of all aspects of Hellerite culture as interpreted by the Seleugon Empire.

KIRK   As this starship's commander, I am empowered to counter any threatening incursion as a violation of intergalactic law.

EPIPHANES   Captain, if the starship Enterprise attempts to intervene, you will suffer the consequences.

MATTATHIAS   You will never subjugate our people!

EPIPHANES   Both you and your confederates must prepare for destruction.

KIRK   Full power deflector screens! Battle stations! Torpedo banks, lock on.

UHURA   Automatic all-points relay from Starfleet Command, Captain, code one.

(The bridge. The starship is rocked by a phaser blast. Sirens commence.)

KIRK   Commence countermeasures!

UHURA   Captain, I've detected a hostile tracking device within the ship!

MATTATHIAS   Aaaaaugh! *(He falls dead.)*

JUDAS   *(Rushing to him)* Father!

MCCOY   Jim! He's dead.

ARISTEAS   Commander Judas, let our forces be joined to avenge this tragedy and free our planet!

(Judas takes Aristeas' hand)

JUDAS   We have no choice but to fight shoulder to shoulder. May the God of old be with us.

KIRK   Calculate orbit of star cruiser now circling. Stand by to fire. Full power.

JUDAS   Captain, I request a communication channel to my base.

KIRK   Of course. Lieutenant Uhura, dedicate a channel for Commander Judas to his planetary base.

UHURA   Yes, Captain.

JUDAS   Hear me, people of Akra! Hear me, people of Alexandria! The Seleugon empire has commenced hostile action against our population. By authority of the Great Kohayn, and by permission of the Hellerite officers, I command you to take up arms and resist the Seleugon forces on the ground and their puppet collaborators, while the Judean coalition takes on their star cruiser!

SPOCK   Captain, our tactical officer has been hit with a guided missile.

JUDAS   I can serve as tactical officer, Captain.

KIRK   Take control of photon torpedoes, Commander, and fire at will.

JUDAS   Aye-aye.

(The Enterprise is rocked again with percussion; the screen shows the Seleugon cruiser being hit by missiles. Finally, it explodes.)

KIRK   How is the tactical officer?

MCCOY   Bruised but satisfactory, Jim.

KIRK   Reports of other casualties?

UHURA   None, Captain.

KIRK   We'll await reports from the planet – Commander, Aristeas, Demetrius, it's safe to return on your shuttlecraft. The Enterprise will stand by if you need any support at Acra.

JUDAS   I thank you for your protection, Captain – and for your diplomacy.

KIRK   It's my honor to assist such an ancient and noble civilization.

(In the passageway)

KIRK   Captain's log, star date 3597.1. The Seleugon empire has retreated from the quadrant, and Acra 168 is at peace. The Vulsids and the Hellerites have achieved a co-existence that is generally cordial, or at least, stable. The Enterprise has completed its mission, and is preparing for departure.

UHURA   Captain, we are receiving a transmission from the command base at Acra. Before we leave, Commander Judas and Aristeas would like to bring a gift. May I permit their shuttlecraft to dock?

KIRK	Of course. It will be nice to see them one more time.

(In the shuttlecraft bay. Enter Judas and Aristeas)

KIRK	Welcome aboard once again. I hope everything is well on the planet?
ARISTEAS	Thank you, Captain, all is well.
JUDAS	We would like to present you with a token of appreciation for what you've done for us. *(Gives him an oil lamp)* This is a vessel from our holy sanctuary – that would still be desecrated, were it not for your assistance.
ARISTEAS	May it light the Enterprise's path on all its voyages.
KIRK	This is very kind of you, gentlemen. We will treasure it, and never forget you.
SPOCK	If I may, I have one question for you.
ARISTEAS	Of course.
SPOCK	I recall that this galaxy is subject to eternal reduplication. In the war against the Seleugons, was the trajectory of history revised? Is your planet doomed to repeat this struggle again and again in the future?
JUDAS	Our fight for liberty was the first of its kind, Mr. Spock. But I regret to say, it won't be the last. Although a new event of history was recorded on Acra, the hearts of people remain as they were. Always seeking more power, always trying to assert the solitary path to righteousness. Although I hope we will never descend to the level of the Seleugons, we are still subject to our passions and frail in our resolve.
ARISTEAS	All we can do is balance humility and pride. And aim to hit the mark of virtue and rectitude.

SPOCK   In this, all the universe's civilizations are the same.

(On the bridge)

KIRK   It's quite a beautiful lamp, wouldn't you say, Mr. Spock?

MCCOY   Don't tease, Jim. You know all notions of beauty are lost on our cold friend.

KIRK   How sad.

SPOCK   Not sad at all, Captain. Sacrificing function for appearance is entirely illogical.

Judah Maccabee's Lonely Hearts Club Band

– a Beatles Hanukkah –

I could do a thorough internet search for evidence of the Beatles' Jewish connections, and I know I would find, or be reminded of, lots of them. So could you. It might be fun.

But the real reason I decided to create a parody of *Yellow Submarine* for Hanukkah is because I think the Seleucid Empire was a lot like the Blue Meanies: oppressive for selfish, egotistical reasons, reveling in crushing those who are different, especially those who dare to object. And there's no better model for spirited resistance than the Fab Four, those adorable characters from Liverpool who never let officious meanies bother them.

And the Lonely Hearts Club Band, as cartoon characters, could do what the Maccabees couldn't: win over the Blue Meanies and convince them to join in the fun.

JOHN
GEORGE
RINGO
PAUL
ZEUS MEANIE
MAX
OLD FRED
ISAIAH JEREMIAH EZEKIEL, PH.D.

JOHN   Once upon a time, or maybe twice, there lay under the sea, an unearthly paradise called Modi'in. The Juice people of Modi'in were happy, for they were governed by the unusual notion that people should take care of each other and live in peace.

GEORGE   Music, joy and love grew in Modi'in – and the Juice people who lived there believed their utopia would last forever.

RINGO   Maybe even longer.

PAUL   There they lived amongst trees that sprouted po- tato latkes, and gentle streams flowing with sour cream cascades.

JOHN   They were as happy as can be.

GEORGE   At first, no one noticed that, on a cliff overlooking the land, a large, fierce, blue, creature was watch- ing them. And this was none other than…

RINGO   Bah – bah –BAAAH!

GEORGE   The Zeus Meanie!

ZEUS MEANIE I *despise* all that Juice happiness, music and love! And I *detest* that silly Juice notion of everyone tak- ing care of each other! These people of Modi'in are an itch on the belly of the universe. They must be scratched! Right, Max?

MAX	Yes, Your Zeusness!
ZEUS MEANIE	*What* did you say, Max? Meanies only take NO for an answer!
MAX	I mean, *no,* Your Zeusness!
ZEUS MEANIE	That's better. Are the pushke-smashers ready?
MAX	No!
ZEUS MEANIE	The flying pigs?
MAX	No!
ZEUS MEANIE	The dreadful Blue Glove?
MAX	No!
ZEUS MEANIE	Splendid! Modi'in, say goodbye to your precious pushkes! Fire!

(Splosh! Choom-choom-choom! Sploosh!)

OLD FRED	The Meanies are coming, the Meanies are coming!
ZEUS MEANIE	What do you see, Max?
MAX	Over there, sir! In the bandstand! The Juices are playing music!
ZEUS MEANIE	We'll soon put an end to that. Blue Glove – smash those instruments and drive away those musicians!

(Thwack! Twang!)

OLD FRED	Aaaaaaugh!
MAX	The Juice people are running away, sir!
ZEUS MEANIE	Good, good. A thing of beauty – destroyed forever. Now we have an empty bandstand. I know what would look perfect in there: a big, lovely, blue statue of ME.

MAX   Wonderful, Your Zeusness!

ZEUS MEANIE   Old man!

OLD FRED   Er – yes?

ZEUS MEANIE   There is to be no more music in your bandstand.
               From now on, all you Juice people will bring deli-
               cious gifts to that statue of ME.

OLD FRED   I don't think so. You see, it's our custom here in
               Modi'in to play music, dance and love each other.

ZEUS MEANIE   Well, your custom is now finished, old man. In the
               past. Defunct.

OLD FRED   You're quite mistaken if you think the Juice people
               are going to accede to your unreasonable and un-
               musical demands.

ZEUS MEANIE   Oh, is that so?

OLD FRED   Quite so.

ZEUS MEANIE   Blue Glove – point at that annoying fellow and
               smash him.

OLD FRED   It's not polite to point. Since I am an officer of the
               British Navy, I suggest it might be more appropri-
               ate to salute – seeing that you're a hand. But that's
               unlikely, so I will just aim this handy cartoon can-
               non at you and –

(Boom!)

               -- promoting myself to Lord Admiral, climb aboard
               the Yellow Submarine and go for help!

JOHN   Go for what?

OLD FRED   Help!

JOHN   You've the wrong script, mate.

GEORGE   Given the circumstances, the place to go would be somewhere with necessary medical support services.

PAUL   You mean, like a blood bank?

GEORGE   No – a Liverpool!

JOHN   Dodging the immense green apples being dropped by the wicked forces of Zeus Meanie, Old Fred sailed across the Sea of Green.

JOHN, PAUL, GEORGE AND RINGO (Melody: "Yellow Submarine")

> In the town where I was born
> Lived a man who sailed the seas
> And he told us of his life
> In the land of Maccabees
>
> So we sailed up to the sun
> Till we found a sea of green
> And we live beneath the waves
> In the town of Modi'in.
>
> We all live in the town of Modi'in, town of Modi'in, town of Modi'in
> We all live in the town of Modi'in, town of Modi'in, town of Modi'in
>
> And our friends are Maccabees
> All Judaical celebrities
> And the band begins to play…
>
> We all live in the town of Modi'in, town of Modi'in, town of Modi'in
> We all live in the town of Modi'in, town of Modi'in, town of Modi'in

OLD FRED   Full speed ahead, Mr. Boatswain, full speed ahead!

JOHN   Full speed ahead it is, Sir.

OLD FRED	Cut the cable, drop the cable!
PAUL	Aye aye, Sir.
GEORGE	Old Fred sailed out of the Sea of Green and up the River Mersey. There he spied a likely lad, and decided to follow him.
RINGO	Woe is me. Liverpool's a lonely place on a Friday evening. I guess I'll stroll over to the Cavern and see what the lads are doing. Wish I could shake the feeling that I'm being followed.
PAUL	Hello, Ringo. What's that yellow submarine behind you, then?
RINGO	I *thought* I was being followed by a yellow submarine. But then I decided it was one of them unidentified flying latkes.
OLD FRED	Ahoy, young mop-top Liverpudlians! Won't you please, please help me?
JOHN	How can we help you, zaydeh?
OLD FRED	First, you must climb aboard this submarine and sail across the sea.
JOHN	What sea? Be pacific.
OLD FRED	Why, the Sea of Green.
PAUL	What if we do?
OLD FRED	It's urgent! The Zeus Meanies have attacked the town of Modi'in, stopped all the music, and installed a big, blue Zeus in the bandstand! Only you can save us.
GEORGE	Why only we?
OLD FRED	Because this is a Beatles movie.

PAUL   But we're not actually the real Beatles. We're just a cartoon version. We're Judah Maccabee's Lonely Hearts Club Band.

JOHN   Nothing is real.

PAUL   Nothing?

JOHN   It's all in the mind, you know.

OLD FRED   None the less, lads, I beg you to come along and save Modi'in from the Zeus Meanies. You're our only hope! And bring your instruments.

RINGO   Your story has touched me heart. Well, then, let's go.

OLD FRED   Fire up those candles over there, drop those chocolate coins in the meter, and we're on our way.

(Vroom!)

GEORGE   All together now!

JOHN, PAUL, GEORGE AND RINGO (Melody: "All Together Now")

One, two, three, four, can I have a little more?
Five, six, seven, eight – that's fine, I love you.

A, B, C, D, We don't need a Christmas tree,
E, F, G, H, I, J – I love you.

Bom bom bom, bompa-bom, light the lights
Bompa-bom, drink your tea
Bompa-bom, spin the top,
Bompa-bom, look at me!

All together now – all together now –
All together now – all together now!

Green, red, black, white, can I have some gelt tonight?
Pink, brown, yellow orange and blue, I love you.

All together now – all together now –
All together now – all together now!

OLD FRED   We're entering the Sea of Time. Plot a course between the Trench of Mystics and the Rational
Ridge.

PAUL   Sounds very philosophical.

OLD FRED   You have to be forty years old to enter the Trench
of Mystics, and none of you lads are over – bless
my beard, but you've all gone old and gray.

JOHN   I feel my mind expanding. Maybe I should put on
a yamulka or something.

OLD FRED   It's because we're in the Sea of Time. Hard to tell
what age we are here.

GEORGE   Look out the window, will you – it's another yellow submarine.

RINGO   Those people are waving at us.

PAUL   Hold on. They look just like us.

OLD FRED   They *are* us. Going the other way through the Sea
of Time.

JOHN   This prompts any number of questions.

JOHN, PAUL, GEORGE AND RINGO (Melody: "When I'm Sixty-Four")

When I get older, losing my hair, many years from
now,
Will you still be chanting the brachot with me,
singing songs of antiquity?
If I should give you another chapeau, would you
lock the door?
Will you still need me, will you still feed me, when
I'm sixty-four?

You'll be older too…

And if you say the word, I could stay with you.

I could be frying sufganiot, while you drink your tea,
Putting on a sweater if the house is cool, Shabbat mornings, drop by the shul.
Spinning a dreidel, winning the gelt, who could ask for more?
Will you still need me, will you still feed me, when I'm sixty-four?

Every winter we can rent a condo in Miami Beach, if it's not too dear,
We shall scrimp and save.
Grandchildren on your knee: Sarah, Scott, and Dave.

Send me a postcard, drop me a line, asking me what's new,
Would it really kill you to pick up a phone – all week long, I sit here alone.
Bring me to meet the whole mishpacha – *ess a bissl* more,
Will you still need me, will you still feed me, when I'm sixty-four.

OLD FRED	The prevailing current has changed. According to my nautical charts, we have entered the Sea of Gornisht.
RINGO	Not much to see here.
(Screech!)	
JOHN	The Yellow Submarine appears to have come to a full stop.
OLD FRED	Gevalt! It's the engine.
PAUL	This couldn't be good.
GEORGE	I don't suppose there's a good mechanic in the Sea

of Gornisht.

RINGO   Why don't you ask him?

JOHN   Whom?

RINGO   That fellow, there.

GEORGE   Where?

PAUL   There's no there here.

RINGO   Oi! Mister!

I.J.EZEKIEL   And are you lost, young troubador, or is it me you're looking for?

GEORGE   We're in need of someone who can fix a submarine engine. Is that something you can help us with?

I.J.EZEKIEL   Though we should keep this entre-nous, there's very little I can't do.

JOHN   Oh, a jack-of-all-trades, are you?

RINGO   Humble little fellow.

OLD FRED   A nebbish.

I.J.EZEKIEL   Lest I should risk a misconstruction, allow my little introduction. I'm Isaiah Jeremiah Ezekiel Phud, a polymath since ere the Flood. In every field, I'm quite a maven, and welcome all to Gornisht Haven.

PAUL   I'm not sure, but I think he speaks English.

I.J.EZEKIEL   I chat in French, Italian, British, Spanish, and a little Yiddish.

GEORGE   Be that as it may, we have a broken-down engine here, and we have to get to Modi'in to fight the Zeus Meanies.

I.J.EZEKIEL   Let's see what made this engine stop. Aha! It needs a little *klop!*

(Bang! Rippetta-rippetta-rippetta-rippetta)

PAUL	If I hadn't seen it with me own eyes.
OLD FRED	We're very much indebted to you, Dr. – eh – Dr. Phud. If you'd like to come along to Modi'in, you're very welcome.
JOHN	That is, unless you want to stay here.
GEORGE	Here? There is no 'here.' We're nowhere. This is the Sea of Gornisht, remember?
I.J.EZEKIEL	You mean, you'd take a nowhere man?
RINGO	Come on. We'll take you somewhere.
I.J.EZEKIEL	Of course, I'd love to take a ride! So let's not wait for time and tide.
OLD FRED	Off we go, then. Everyone inside? We voyage next through the Torah Sea. Ringo, please be careful reaching outside the vessel. You won't be much of a drummer if you lose an arm.
RINGO	Look, I've caught a tiny little Torah.
JOHN	Take care of that, Ringo, it's very important.
RINGO	I'll just keep it here. Look! I have a scroll in me pocket.
PAUL	Isn't that Modi'in up ahead?
GEORGE	It's very colorful.
JOHN	Almost psychedelic.
RINGO	Unreal.

JOHN, PAUL, GEORGE AND RINGO (Melody: "Lucy in the Sky with Diamonds")

Picture yourself with a grated potato
With apple-sauce trees and sour cream skies
Somebody calls you, you answer quite slowly
With words you can't rationalize –
Tiny wax candles of yellow and green
Tell you to cover your head
Reach for a match but it opens its wings and it's gone –

Nes gadol haya sham, nes gadol haya sham,
Nes gadol haya sham, aaaaahhhh –

Follow it down to a train in a station
Where Israelite people eat corn beef on rye
Everyone smiles as you float past the platform
Conversing with macaroon pie
Matza ball bicycles drift through the sky
Bringing you kasha and hay
Look for some seltzer to wash it all down, and you're gone –

Nes gadol haya sham, nes gadol haya sham,
Nes gadol haya sham, aaaaahhhh –

OLD FRED   We've arrived. You can see poor, colorless, music-less Modi'in.

JOHN   This is so terribly sad.

PAUL   The Zeus Meanies have taken over Modi'in – trouncing Torah, shmeissing Shabbes, menacing mensches, and worst of all, klopping klezmers!

GEORGE   How can we stop them?

OLD FRED   With music. They can't bear it! They shrink at the sound of music!

JOHN   We should have brought along Rodgers and

Hammerstein then.

PAUL   Let's get our instruments out of steerage and go after them!

MAX   Your Zeusness, look! It's the band!

ZEUS MEANIE   What band, grimy little Max?

MAX   Coming out of that submarine! It's Judah Maccabee's Lonely Hearts Club Band!

ZEUS MEANIE   Aaaagh! My mortal enemies! Music, love, peace, laughter – everything I despise! Glovey, lock and load.

OLD FRED   We'll have to draw their fire on one front, and sneak up on another.

RINGO   Lucky we have these cardboard cutouts of ourselves.

PAUL   Where'd you find those?

RINGO   The animation studio left them behind.

JOHN   Brillant! Set them up here, and – can cardboard cutouts play music?

I.J.EZEKIEL   A task like this you can hand to me; I'll rig up a bagpipe calliope!

GEORGE   That should do the trick.

ZEUS MEANIE   Glove, take aim at that Judah Maccabee band and *fire!*

(Boom!)

MAX   You got him, sir! He fell right over!

ZEUS MEANIE   Call out the apple-bonkers!

MAX   Apple-bonkers – advance!

JOHN   Now that's something you don't see every day.
                Grown men in uniform making applesauce.

MAX   Fire!

(Bonk, bonk, bonk, splat!)

GEORGE   Tasty. Wish we had some latkes.

ZEUS MEANIE   It's strange, Max, but I think I hear bagpipes.

MAX   Sir, look behind you!

GEORGE   Cheers, you big blue Zeus. We'd like to play you a
                reprise. Lads? One, two, one-two-three-four –

JOHN, PAUL, GEORGE AND RINGO (Melody: "All Together Now")

                One, two, three, four, can I have a little more?
                Five, six, seven, eight – that's fine, I love you.

                A, B, C, D, We don't need a Christmas tree,
                E, F, G, H, I, J – I love you.

                Bom bom bom, bompa-bom, light the lights
                Bompa-bom, drink your tea
                Bompa-bom, spin the top,
                Bompa-bom, look at me!

                All together now – all together now –
                All together now – all together now!

OLD FRED   By Neptune's knickerbockers, all the color's com-
                ing back!

JOHN   The Zeus Meanies are fleeing in terror!

GEORGE   With their flying blue glove and their anti-music
                missiles.

RINGO   Leaving all this lovely applesauce.

I.J.EZEKIEL   A splendid ending to the strife, as Modi'in comes
                back to life!

PAUL   Now Modi'in can restore itself to its former glory. May music, love, friendship and peace reign in its hills and fields.

OLD FRED   Ringo, that scroll you have in your pocket …

RINGO   This?

OLD FRED   Yes, do you think you could part with it? The Zeus Meanies took all our Torah scrolls away. We really can't do without them.

RINGO   Of course. Happy to oblige. Here you are.

OLD FRED   In gratitude to Judah Maccabee's Lonely Hearts Club Band, the people of Modi'in have asked me to present to you this psychedelic dreidel. It has four sides, one for each of you, and it will bring you fame, fortune and adulation wherever you go.

I.J.EZEKIEL   But first, you should be made aware, look what's transpiring over there!

ZEUS MEANIE   *(sadly)* Oh, Max. What will become of us? It's no longer a blue world, Max. Where will we go?

MAX   Sir, I fear there's no place for us any longer.

JOHN   Hello over there, blue people? Why don't you come join us? And then the world will be as one.

PAUL   It's a rainbow world in Modi'in, and we can't do without blue.

GEORGE   It'll be ever so much nicer if you'll stay.

ZEUS MEANIE   You want us … to stay?

I.J.EZEKIEL   It would be a lovely ending, with a diplomatic friending.

RINGO   You may as well, you know. Even with the music and all. You might even start to like it.

PAUL   You can be in charge of the blues!

ZEUS MEANIE   Well then ... since you put it that way ... Max and I
                accept!

GEORGE   That's what we like to hear!

ALL   All together now, all together now, all together
                now, all together NOW!

A Hanukkah Song

– the Charles Dickens revision –

Look at Fagin, Uriah Heep, and Barney the Jew. Bad guys from the classic Victorian English writer, Charles Dickens. They're miserly, unsympathetic, and cruel, they are enemies of all that is beloved and good.

I love *A Christmas Carol*. It's one of the most perfectly-written works of the English language. But Ebenezer Scrooge – Dickens may have been using the Hebrew first name as a code for Jew here, too -- is another miserly antagonist, albeit one with child-hood Christmas memories. I decided to face this squarely. I grabbed him, re-named him Eliezer Shmooze, made him a debt collector and plunked him down in contemporary New York City as Hanukkah approaches.

ELIEZER SHMOOZE, A DEBT COLLECTOR
NARRATOR
BOB KRAVITZ, SHMOOZE'S ASSISTANT
FRED, THE SYNAGOGUE PRESIDENT
MARVIN JACOBS, SHMOOZE'S FORMER PARTNER
GHOST OF HANUKKAH PAST
GHOST OF HANUKKAH PRESENT
MRS. KRAVITZ
LITTLE LENNY
UNDERTAKER

SHMOOZE   Marvin was dead, to begin with. At least he was dead to *me;* he filed his retirement application with the Social Security Administration, closed up his apartment, signed over his partnership agreement and moved to Boca Raton. As his sole friend and heir, I took the old mamzer to the airport, told him "zolst lign in drerd," and dropped him off at terminal three. Thus Marvin left me to run this miserable collection agency alone.

NARRATOR   Shmooze never painted out old Marvin's name on the glass of their office door. There it remained, years afterward: "Shmooze and Marvin Receivables." And in that office, Shmooze continued the wretched business of buying up debt and hounding non-payers into submission. Oh, but he was a tightfisted, miserly cheapskate, was old Eliezer Shmooze! Hard as flint, and solitary as a vulture, he carried winter with him like a cloak as he strode between his boarding house on the West Side to the agency above a decrepit bodega on First Avenue.

BOB KRAVITZ   Nobody ever stopped him on the street with a friendly, "Eliezer, *vos macht a yid?*" No schnorrers begged him for a quarter, no child asked him for the time. Even blind men seemed to sense his approach, and crossed the street at great risk to life and limb. For me, however, it wasn't so easy to avoid Mr. Shmooze. I was his assistant, and sat day after day crouched over a little desk in the agency, typing collection letters with frostbitten fingers. Mr. Shmooze never set the thermostat above fifty degrees.

NARRATOR It was a cold morning in late December when the creaky office door opened and Shmooze entered, glaring at Bob Kravitz.

BOB KRAVITZ Good morning, Mr. Shmooze!

SHMOOZE Bah! What's so good about it? Get on with your work, Bob Kravitz.

NARRATOR And a moment later, in came Fred, the amiable, rotund synagogue president, stomping his cold feet and blowing on his hands.

FRED Sholom aleichem, Eliezer! And a happy Hanukkah to you.

SHMOOZE Such *narishkeit*. Away with you, Fred.

FRED Hanukkah is *narishkeit*, Eliezer? You don't mean that, I'm sure.

SHMOOZE I do. 'Happy Hanukkah'! Feh! What reason have you to be happy? You're poor enough.

FRED Nu, what reason have you to be miserable, Eliezer? You're rich enough! Don't be grouchy. I've come to bring you greetings of the season, and to learn what pledge you'd like to make to the annual cemetery fund drive.

SHMOOZE Pledge? None!

FRED No pledge to the cemetery fund, then? Perhaps, at this festive time of year, you'd prefer to make your contribution to the Hebrew school improvement campaign?

SHMOOZE   A plague on the Hebrew school.

FRED   Eliezer, it's at this cold and dark time of year that we make some provision for poor shlemiels who are in want of common necessities, and can't afford cemetery maintenance fees and bar-mitsva tutors.

SHMOOZE   Are there no Chabad houses?

FRED   Well, yes, there are, but ...

SHMOOZE   And the Hebrew Free Burial Association, is it still in operation?

FRED   It is, Eliezer, but that exists for ...

SHMOOZE   United Way and the Salvation Army are in full vigor, still?

FRED   Very busy, I'm sorry to say, Eliezer. But, tell me, how much should I put you down for?

SHMOOZE   Nothing! I wish to be left alone. If the *shnorrers* don't want to make use of those institutions, then let them quit and decrease the synagogue population. And I would advise you to mind your own business and not to interfere with other people's. Good day!

NARRATOR   Seeing that it would be useless to continue the conversation, the synagogue president left the office. Bob Kravitz continued his gloomy task of harassing debtors, while outside, holiday sounds drifted up to the grimy office window but scarcely dared to petition for entrance. As the sun began to descend over the Hudson River, Shmooze looked at his assistant and said:

SHMOOZE   You'll want to go home early, and light Hanukkah candles, I suppose?

BOB KRAVITZ   If it's convenient, sir.

SHMOOZE   It's not at all convenient, and it's not fair. If I docked you an hour's pay, you'd consider yourself ill-used, wouldn't you?

BOB KRAVITZ   Well, Hanukkah comes but once a year, sir.

SHMOOZE   For eight days it does! A poor excuse for picking a man's pocket. But if you must leave early, then go. Be here all the earlier tomorrow morning.

NARRATOR   Bob promised he would, and left Shmooze to finish the day's threatening phone calls and close up the office. He went down the stairs, and after scowling at the bodega clerk, Shmooze took his dollar-menu dinner at McDonald's and thence home to bed. His room was as cold as his office, and he pulled his thrift-store comforter well up under his chin. A car alarm in the street kept him awake for a while, but at last Shmooze fell asleep.

MARVIN   Eliezer!

SHMOOZE   What! What! Who's there?

MARVIN   Eliezer!

SHMOOZE   Where are you? Who are you?

MARVIN   You should ask me who I *was*. I was your partner, Marvin Jacobs.

SHMOOZE   Marvin! But you've been gone seven long years. And you gave back your key!

MARVIN   Ah, you don't believe in me. Do you doubt your senses?

SHMOOZE   My senses? They are fooled by a slight disorder of the stomach. A *krenk in kishkes*. You're not really here; you're just an undigested bit of nova lox.

MARVIN   Do not kid me, Eliezer. You are far too cheap to spring for nova lox. We have very little time. I come to warn you to avoid my fate. Seven years I have walked the small confines of a dismal Florida condo, devoid of friends, of colleagues, of anyone who thinks of me fondly.

SHMOOZE   Marvin – Marvin, are those chains you wear about your neck?

MARVIN   I wear the chains I bought in the diamond district. I treasured them instead of the goodwill of my fellow men. Would that I had spent their price to relieve the suffering of the poor, the lame, and the homeless!

NARRATOR   And Marvin let out a cry of such piteous distress to rend the heart of any living soul.

MARVIN   Aaaaaooooughhh!

SHMOOZE   You were such a sharp man of business, Marvin. This should be a comfort to you.

MARVIN   Mankind was my business, Eliezer! *Tsedokeh* and *rachmoness* were my business! Mark my words. I bring not comfort, but a warning. If you would not walk my path for all eternity, take heed. You still have a chance to escape my doom.

Tonight, you will be haunted by three spirits. Without these visits, you cannot hope to shun my fate. Expect the first when the bell tolls one. The second, at the strike of two. The third, at three. Take heed! Take heeeeeed! Farewell.

NARRATOR   And Marvin Jacobs, walking backwards, passed insubstantially through the wall of Shmooze's room. He was left alone, stunned, trembling, and afraid.

SHMOOZE   It was only a dream. It wasn't real. Marvin never talked so *meshuggeh*. I'm not going to let this upset me. I'm going back to sleep right now and forget all about –

NARRATOR   Just then the bell struck one.

(Bong!)

SHMOOZE   Oy.

NARRATOR   The curtains of his bed were drawn aside, and
Shmooze, starting up into a half-recumbent position, found himself face to face with an unearthly
visitor – a strange figure, draped in a luminous
veil. It glowed as it floated in mid-air, and resem-
bled nothing so much as ghostly, translucent
chicken.

SHMOOZE   Are you the spirit, sir, whose coming was foretold
to me?

G. O. H. PAST   I am that spirit, Eliezer Shmooze -- the Ghost of
Hanukkah Past.

SHMOOZE   Long past, spirit?

G. O. H. PAST   No. *Your* past. I have come here in the interest of
your welfare. Rise, take my wing, and come with
me!

NARRATOR   The visitor's grasp, gentle as a woman's hand, was
not to be resisted. Passing through the unopened
window, the pair floated over the city streets. The
misty darkness vanished, and Shmooze found himself standing by the chicken's side in front of an ancient synagogue not far from the Battery.

SHMOOZE   *Gottenyu!* I grew up in this shul! I was a boy here!
It was demolished years ago. Spirit, lead me where
you will.

NARRATOR   The spirit led him through the battered front doors,
past the memorial plaques in the hall, and into the
modest sanctuary. Shmooze saw young boys in ill-
fitting suits sitting in the pews, and heard, as if

from a distance, the chanting of a cantor.

G. O. H. PAST   It is here, Eliezer, that you became a bar mitsva; on that bimah you stood and chanted your Torah portion, and spoke movingly of God's commandment to repair a broken world, to feed the hungry and care for the sick. In this very row sat lovely young Blanche Weinberg, watching you with shining eyes. And there, nearest the pulpit, sat your loving parents, *kvelling* and and hopeful of the glorious adulthood that lay ahead for you.

SHMOOZE   Ah, look at my parents – so long gone. And Blanche – how well I remember her. She was kind, and ... gentle ...

G. O. H. PAST   What is the matter?

SHMOOZE   Nothing, except ... I wish I had been more generous, yesterday, to my synagogue president when he asked me to support the Hebrew school campaign.

G. O. H. PAST   You did not remain to attend confirmation class, did you, Eliezer?

SHMOOZE   No. I left after bar mitsva. And now I bitterly regret the loss of my schoolmates, the best friends a boy could ever have.

G. O. H. PAST   Come with me once more, and look into this factory window. What do you see?

SHMOOZE   Why, this is my father's candy factory! And there he sits with his head in his hands ...

G. O. H. PAST   You know the cause of his melancholy.

SHMOOZE   Yes, spirit. To my deep shame, I know. He mourns because I just refused to join the family business. Instead, I went away to work for a loan shark ... on Staten Island ... such a *shondeh* ...

G. O. H. PAST   Do you see that lone figure, on the bench across the street, sobbing as the snow falls around her?

SHMOOZE   My beloved Blanche, my sweet, innocent Blanche. Such a *shayna meydl.* I broke her devoted heart when I left. But she never said an unkind word to me. How I wish … ah, well, it's all in the past. Spirit! No more! Why do you delight to torture me? Take me home, spirit, show me no more!

G. O. H. PAST   These are but the shadows of things that have been, Eliezer. That they are thus, do not blame me.

SHMOOZE   Take me home, spirit, haunt me no longer!

NARRATOR   With a reproachful cluck, the apparition took Shmooze's hand and pulled him outside, up into the night sky, and led him back to his boarding house. He fell, sobbing, into his bed, and was thus lying in semi-consciousness when the bell struck two.

(Bong! Bong!)

G. O. H. PRESENT   Eliezer Shmooze! Arise!

NARRATOR   Standing by Shmooze's bed was a towering spectre, clothed in voluminous robes, a breastplate and helmet, and holding a shield. Its piercing eyes fixed him with a stern yet humorous gaze.

SHMOOZE   Are you the second spirit I was told to expect?

G. O. H. PRESENT   Yes. I am the Ghost of Hanukkah Present. You have never seen the like of me before.

SHMOOZE   You seem to be a figure from long ago.

G. O. H. PRESENT   I came into this world only this afternoon. Each year, for twenty-two centuries, the Maccabee spirit is born anew, when our people remember the struggle for freedom, and re-light the flame of dedication to a proud heritage. Yet you, Eliezer, have stubbornly refused to partake in this sacred commemoration.

SHMOOZE   It's a regret that weighs heavy on me, this remarkable night.

G. O. H. PRESENT   I have much to teach you, Eliezer. Touch my robe!

NARRATOR   Shmooze did so, and held on fast. Together they rose through the air and glided through the wall of the decrepit boarding house. The cold stars lit their path toward Riverdale, where gently they landed before a small apartment building on a twisted side street littered with trash. In many of the windows, sparkling Hanukkah menorahs proudly held up the first candle of the festival of liberation.

G. O. H. PRESENT   Look into this window, Eliezer Shmooze. Do you recognize the family within?

NARRATOR   Through the icy window nearest the building entrance, Shmooze spied a stout housewife, flanked by several excited children, carrying into the dining room a large covered platter. The room was festively hung with paper dreidels and colored ribbons, and the matron beamed as she ushered her children to their chairs.

SHMOOZE   I think that might be Bob Kravitz's wife.

MRS. KRAVITZ   Bob! Bob, come in already, or you'll miss the latkes!

BOB KRAVITZ   Here I am, dear. Oh, that does smell good! Laura, there's no one in New York who can cook such wonderful latkes.

MRS. KRAVITZ   Little Lenny, please bring out the applesauce.

LITTLE LENNY   Sure, Mom!

MRS. KRAVITZ   (whispering) Bob, did you bring home the ...

BOB KRAVITZ   I did what I could, my dear. The prices have gone up since last year.

MRS. KRAVITZ   If that old miser could bring himself just once to give you a bonus, we wouldn't have to scrape at Hanukkah time.

BOB KRAVITZ   He is what he is, Laura. Nothing I can do is going to change him. We have to cope as best we can.

MRS. KRAVITZ   It's going to be especially hard this year. The landlord put flyers under all the doors this morning. He was granted permission to de-regulate the building at the end of the tenants' current leases.

BOB KRAVITZ   *Vey iz mir!* No more rent stabilization?

MRS. KRAVITZ   No, unfortunately. When the lease is up, we'll have to find another apartment. And it seems certain that higher rent means that the children will have to go to public school next fall.

LITTLE LENNY   What did you say, Mom? We're going to public school?

MRS. KRAVITZ   It's very possible, Little Lenny, if we have to move. I'm so sorry.

LITTLE LENNY   Don't worry, Mom! I can make new friends! It will be okay!

BOB KRAVITZ   Such a precious, sunny, happy little boy. As good as gold.

LITTLE LENNY   As long as we all have each other, everything will be fine, Dad!

BOB KRAVITZ   That's right, son. As long as we all have each other, nothing is too hard to bear. Wait! Is that the door? Are Bubbie and Zayde here?

NARRATOR   Unconscious of the ghostly presence of Shmooze and his guiding spirit, the Kravitz relatives crowded past them into the brightly-lit apartment.

LITTLE LENNY   Bubbie! Zayde! You're just in time for dinner and there's *such* a brisket!

MRS. KRAVITZ   Come sit down, everyone, before dinner gets cold. And, children, if you look under your plates you'll find your Hanukkah presents!

LITTLE LENNY   Some chocolate gelt.

BOB KRAVITZ   A blessing on your dear heads, children.

LITTLE LENNY   God help us, every one.

SHMOOZE   Spirit, tell me, I beg you. Tell me whether Little Lenny will have to go to public school.

G. O. H. PRESENT   I see a vacant seat at the Dalton School, and a backpack without an owner, carefully preserved. If these shadows remain unaltered by the Future, these children will be enrolled in city schools at this time next year. Their synagogue dues will go unpaid and they will not be scheduled for b'nai mitsva.

SHMOOZE   No, no, kind Spirit! Say they will be spared!

G. O. H. PRESENT   What then? If this is to be, let them drop out, then, and reduce the synagogue population.

NARRATOR   Shmooze hung his head to hear his own words quoted by the spirit, and was overcome with shame and grief.

BOB KRAVITZ   Hear, hear! Raise your glasses, everyone. Let's drink the good health of Mr. Shmooze, the founder of the feast. L'chaim!

MRS. KRAVITZ   Founder of the feast, is he? I'd like to give him a *potch* to feast on.

BOB KRAVITZ   My dear, the children! It's Hanukkah!

MRS. KRAVITZ I'll drink his health for your sake, not his. L'chaim.

NARRATOR The Spirit took Shmooze's hand and lifted him back up above the street, and they floated gently, silently, over the wintry city. It was with a new eye that Shmooze looked upon the homeless figures huddled in doorways, and the solitary bus passengers gazing out into the night.

SHMOOZE Those poor and lonely people, Spirit – have they no refuge or resource?

G. O. H. PRESENT Is there no Salvation Army? Is the Hebrew Free Burial Society still in operation?

(Bong! Bong! Bong!)

NARRATOR The bell struck three just as the spirit faded into the night. In his place Shmooze made out a terrifying figure – just a hooded cloak, which stood before him without face or hands.

SHMOOZE Are you the third spirit who was foretold?

NARRATOR Silently, the spirit nodded.

SHMOOZE I fear I know you, spirit. You have come to tell me the future, which I tremble to learn.

NARRATOR The ghostly figure nodded again, and with unseen hand beckoned him to follow. They rode the bitter cold wind down the West Side Highway and descended to the pavement in daylight before the Riverside Memorial Chapel. There, two bundled-up figures stood in front of the wide brass doors. The spirit pointed at them.

UNDERTAKER There doesn't seem to be any point in waiting. No one from the shul is here; none of his neighbors; not his old partner, Marvin.

FRED And the rabbi had an important ritual committee meeting.

UNDERTAKER   I may as well put the visitor register away, and head out to the cemetery. Are you coming along?

FRED   It doesn't seem right to send him to the grave alone – even an old *mamzer* like Shmooze.

SHMOOZE   Like Shmooze! It's me they're talking about! It's me in the coffin!

UNDERTAKER   Look at that old woman with the shopping cart! She was the same one standing by his door when we carried him out. It looks like she's taken his blankets. Oh! There's his hat and coat, too. Well, they can't keep him warm now.

FRED   Here comes Bob Kravitz and his wife. Hello, friends, it's good to see you, even under the circumstances.

BOB KRAVITZ   We couldn't let Mr. Shmooze go without at least saying goodbye.

UNDERTAKER   Well, you're the only ones.

MRS. KRAVITZ   It's likely a lot of poor debtors will feel relief at his passing.

BOB KRAVITZ   Yes, he was a hard man to those who owed money.

MRS. KRAVITZ   A hard man to everyone, you mean. You suffered worse by him than anyone on his collection list.

UNDERTAKER   Be that as it may, it's over now. Death cancels all sins.

FRED   True. Well, *zey gezundt,* my friends. I have to get back to the shul. We're setting up for the Hanukkah party.

BOB KRAVITZ   Happy Hanukkah.

MRS. KRAVITZ   Rest in peace, you lousy old miser.

SHMOOZE   Spirit! This is a fearful place. I swear I won't forget its lesson! Please, take me away from here! But first, tell me: are these the shadows of things that *will* be, or are they shadows of things that *may* be, only?

NARRATOR   The grim spectre pointed to Shmooze's name spelled out on the marquee of the memorial chapel.

SHMOOZE   But why show me all this, if I'm beyond hope? Spirit, tell me I might still sponge away the writing on this sign! Please! Please!

NARRATOR   And Shmooze clung to the ghostly sleeve, sobbing, begging, for any sliver of hope that he might redeem himself. But the spirit of Hanukkah Past remained silent and pitiless, as the day faded to dark, and the sleeve – transformed itself to a bedsheet. Shmooze found he was kneeling on the floor in his room, as the bright morning light streamed through his window.

SHMOOZE   What – what is this? My bed! My blanket – still here! I'm alive! *Baruch hashem,* I've been spared. I've been given another chance! Spirits – thank you all! I won't waste it. I'm a new man! Am I laughing or crying, I'm all *farmisht!* Is it morning? Have the spirits done it all in one night? Is it still the first day of Hanukkah?

NARRATOR   The newly-awakened man ran to his window and threw it open.

SHMOOZE   Hello, down there, hello! You! Boy! Is that you, Little Lenny?

LITTLE LENNY   Is that – is that – Mr. Shmooze?

SHMOOZE   Clever boy, sensible boy! Yes, Little Lenny, it's me, Mr. Shmooze! But don't be afraid. I promise you, I'm a mensch now! Such a night I've had! Wait for me while I come down, Little Lenny, I've a lovely surprise for you and your family. Can you keep a secret?

LITTLE LENNY Well, yes, sir, if you like.

NARRATOR   And the boy waited in confusion as Shmooze pulled on his clothes and fairly danced down the stairs to the street.

SHMOOZE   My fine young friend, we're going to give your parents something wonderful. Do you know whether that great brownstone on Gramercy Park, the one that had the realtor's sign hanging outside?

LITTLE LENNY What, the sign as big as me?

SHMOOZE   A delightful little fellow. Yes, dear boy!

LITTLE LENNY It's hanging there now.

SHMOOZE   Come with me, Little Lenny. I'm going to buy that house right now and your whole *mishpoche* can move right in, and live there for the rest of your days.

LITTLE LENNY How is it by you, Mr. Shmooze? Are you feeling okay?

SHMOOZE   Little Lenny, I never felt better in my life! But first, *boychik*, I'll ask you to walk with me to the shul. I have something to tell the president. And, on the way back to your apartment, I think we'll be passing F.A.O. Schwartz, won't we?

LITTLE LENNY Yes, we will, Mr. Shmooze.

SHMOOZE   And that's very convenient, Little Lenny, because we're going to stop in there so you can pick out Hanukkah presents for your brothers and sisters, and for your parents, and of course a very nice one for yourself, too.

LITTLE LENNY Mr. Shmooze! What a *mechaya!* Do you really mean it?

SHMOOZE   I'll be as good as my word, young friend. Ah, here we are at the shul. Maybe we'll find him here at this busy season of the year. Ah! Fred! A *freyliche Hanikkeh* to you, sir.

FRED   Eliezer Shmooze? Is that you?

SHMOOZE   Yes, Fred, it's me, to humbly ask your pardon for my past rudeness. I hope you'll accept my pledge to the cemetery fund and the Hebrew school improvement campaign. Here's my credit card, and I'd like you to charge *(whispers)*.

FRED   Eliezer! Great heavens, are you serious?

SHMOOZE   Please don't say another word. That amount includes a great many back payments. I look forward to seeing you on Shabbat, and I'd like the honor of sponsoring the Kiddush, if I may?

FRED   A blessing on your head, Eliezer.

SHMOOZE   Well, Little Lenny, that's done. Now, we have some business to attend to, don't we? I'm not sure we'll be able to carry all those packages! Let's hire a horse and carriage to take us uptown.

LITTLE LENNY   Thank you, Mr. Shmooze! This is the best day of my life!

SHMOOZE   Ah, thank *you*, my good fellow. This is the best day of *my* life, too.

NARRATOR   And Eliezer Shmooze was as good as his word. To the Kravitz family, he became a favorite uncle. In the synagogue, he was a beloved pillar. And among the city's philanthropists, his was an honored name.

Never did he forget the lessons he learned during that long Hanukkah night. Our task here in this

life is to work for the repair of the world, and to relieve the burdens of our fellows when we can. To
this task, Eliezer Shmooze dedicated himself entirely on the festival of miracles. As he brought
light into the lives of others, may we also be in-
spired to climb to ever-higher summits of repen-
tance and atonement, and become a blessing. May
that be truly said of us, and all of us. And so, as
Little Lenny observed, God help us, every one!

Rabbi Shoshana Hantman grew up in the West Mount Airy section of Philadelphia, and was educated at Gratz College and the University of Pennsylvania. She received ordination from the Reconstructionist Rabbinical College, and a master's degree in education from Temple University. Shoshana has served as both a congregational rabbi and a synagogue education director; in 1992, she founded the independent Halutsim Hebrew School, where the students read plays in class nearly every week. Shoshana lives in northern Westchester County, New York, with her husband Richard Weill and their two children. Her first book, *Passover Parodies: Short Plays for the Seder Table,* was awarded a Gold Medal at the 2014 Independent Publishers Book Awards. Her second book, *Choose Your Path: Adventures in American Jewish History*, was a 2018 Independent Publishers Book Awards Silver Medal Winner.

www.ingramcontent.com/pod-product-compliance
Lightning Source LLC
Chambersburg PA
CBHW030156070426
42447CB00031B/474